DOMESTICK PRIVACIES

Domestick Privacies

SAMUEL JOHNSON
and the
ART OF BIOGRAPHY

EDITED BY
DAVID WHEELER

THE UNIVERSITY PRESS OF KENTUCKY

Copyright © 1987 by The University Press of Kentucky
Scholarly publisher for the Commonwealth,
serving Bellarmine College, Berea College, Centre
College of Kentucky, Eastern Kentucky University,
The Filson Club, Georgetown College, Kentucky
Historical Society, Kentucky State University,
Morehead State University, Murray State University,
Northern Kentucky University, Transylvania University,
University of Kentucky, University of Louisville,
and Western Kentucky University.

Editorial and sales Offices: Lexington, Kentucky 40506-0024

Library of Congress Cataloging in Publication Data

Domestick privacies.

Bibliography: p.
Includes index.
1. Johnson, Samuel, 1709-1784—Criticism and
interpretation.   2. Biography (as a literary form)
I. Wheeler, David, 1950-
PR3537.B54D66   1987   828'.609   87-10547
ISBN 0-8131-1612-0

CONTENTS

ACKNOWLEDGMENTS

Many friends and colleagues offered valuable suggestions and encouragement at various stages of this project, and I owe gratitude to John Burke, Edward Tomarken, Fredric Bogel, John Middendorf, W.C. Dowling, Thomas Curley, Tom Kaminski, Frederick Keener, Jeane Brink, John Abbott, Gwin Kolb, Ralph Rader, Paul Alkon, Richard Wendorf, Paul Korshin, Albrecht Strauss, Mark Booth, and Thomas Bonnell. Special thanks go to Robert Folkenflik for the sound advice and help he provided from the inception.

I owe a special debt to my teachers at Chicago and Virginia—Edward Rosenheim, Arthur Friedman, Sheldon Sacks, Leo Damrosch, and Martin Battestin—who taught me about the eighteenth century; to the late Irvin Ehrenpreis whose Johnson seminar marked the beginning; and especially to Ralph Cohen who, like Johnson, always questioned.

I wish to thank my colleagues at the University of Southern Mississippi—Tom Richardson, Gary Stringer, Philip Kolin, Kim Herzinger, Maureen Ryan, David Roberts, Fredric Dolezal, and Rex Stamper—who read essays and gave advice and support; Dean Terry Harper for his continued support of my work; and my wife, Marjorie Spruill Wheeler, for the special quality of hers.

Finally, I thank the contributors for their patience and their cooperation. It is, after all, their book.

DAVID   WHEELER

Introduction: The Uses of Johnson's Biographies

John J. Burke, Jr., begins the introduction to his recent collection of essays on Johnson, *The Unknown Samuel Johnson*, with a series of worthy questions: "How can we speak of an 'unknown' Johnson? Is he not one of the best-known names in English literature? Would it not make more sense to speak of an 'unknown' Chaucer? Or, even better, of an 'unknown' Shakespeare?"[1] Clearly all three of these writers are "known" by just about every educated reader of English. Burke's questions are worth asking, however, because of the different way in which these authors are known. The general reader knows Chaucer because he knows *The Canterbury Tales*; he knows Shakespeare because he knows the plays and perhaps the sonnets. Chaucer's and Shakespeare's works are read frequently and repeatedly, but Johnson's works are not; it is likely, therefore, that the reader knows Johnson not as an author, like Chaucer and Shakespeare, but as a "literary figure," as the subject of Boswell's biography, arguably the best-known biography in our possession. Nonspecialists view Johnson, the master stylist, critic, moralist, biographer, as Boswell depicted him, a living legend stomping around London, giant walking stick in hand, bluster and wit rolling off his tongue, ready to put down Lord Chesterfield, Bishop Berkeley, a female preacher, and anyone daring to engage him in debate. *Doctor* Johnson: the honorary title, like Lord Jim's, signifies the legend.

But, necessarily, the writer preceded the legend. Before he was Doctor Johnson, he wrote the *Life of Savage*; before he was "Dictionary Johnson," he wrote the *Rambler*. Because of the legend, we might associate Johnson with biography (at least as the subject of biography); but unless we are students of Johnson or of biography, we tend to ignore Boswell's opening— "to write the Life of him who excelled all mankind in writing the lives of others"—and often overlook Johnson's own work as biographer.[2] Johnson's canon, of course, includes nearly every literary form or genre imaginable, but he was a biographer from start to finish, from the hacked out *Life of Father Paul Sarpi* to the consummate *Lives of the Poets*. And as he did with the periodic, moral, political, and literary essay, Johnson left his large imprint on biography, which, despite its long history of development, was, by our standards, still an embryonic form in the eighteenth century.

Because biography holds a central place in Johnson's canon and because biography (especially autobiography) was, by his own admission, Johnson's favorite genre, I suggest (as does William Siebenschuh in an essay that follows) that Johnson's biographical writings—or perhaps "life writings" is a more accurate term—provide a particularly apt place to "know" Johnson.

Why was Johnson so attracted to life writing? "No species of writing," Johnson writes in *Rambler* 60, "seems more worthy of cultivation than biography, since none can be more delightful or more useful, none can more certainly enchain the heart by irresistible interest, or more widely diffuse instruction to every diversity of condition."[3] Biography, then, accomplishes the dual end of literature. It delights the soul by creating a chain of sympathy between subject and reader, and it instructs the mind by providing behavioral examples: Francis Drake, exemplifying courage and decisiveness in an era when heroes were more plentiful and heroism more possible, offers a model; Charles XII of Sweden, exemplifying military genius

turned tyrant, offers a warning. For Johnson and other eighteenth-century writers, life writing, in providing such examples, is useful not only as a distinguishable mode of discourse
in full-fledged "biographies" (the appealing but excessive Savage wastes his potential and his life; the bookish Gray writes
poetry derived from isolated thought rather than sound experience) but also as an identifiable component of other literary
modes.

Biographical elements appear not only in Johnson's biographies and diaries but also in those writings we might, for lack
of a better, inclusive term, label "imaginative." The better-
known poems, *Rasselas*, and *Irene* all contain biographical
sections or adopt a form we associate with biography. Based on
what Johnson thought was historical fact, Irene's behavior
leads to predictable consequences and can serve as instruction. Johnson's three most familiar poems, the only three, in
fact, anthologized with any regularity—*London, The Vanity of
Human Wishes*, and *On the Death of Dr. Robert Levet*—depend,
to an increasing extent, on biographical materials. *London*
focuses on the biographical moment, the departure from London of a supposedly fictional character, as an opportunity for
topical commentary about the conditions necessitating the
departure. The most interesting of these poems in a biographical context, *The Vanity of Human Wishes*, presents a gallery of
mini-lives designed to illustrate the essential futility of expecting earthly happiness. In its manner of presentation it resem-
bles Pope's *To a Lady: Of the Characters of Women* (Moral Essay
II), though, of course, its central idea is far more serious. *Levet*
is Johnsonian biography on its smallest scale, stripped bare: a
few, character-forming details from the life—"Officious, inno-
cent, sincere, / of ev'ry friendless name the friend": the well-
employed single talent—and the moral lesson to be drawn
from them.

The History of Rasselas, Prince of Abyssinia is a "life history,"
but more memorable, perhaps, than Rasselas's life story, of
which we see only a portion, are the set-piece biographies of
Imlac (chapters 8–12) and the mad astronomer (chapters
40–46). These sections of the work remind us of similar inter-

polated narratives in Fielding—Mr. Wilson's life story in *Joseph Andrews* or the Man of the Hill section of *Tom Jones*, for example—and they are used in approximately the same way: to provide object moral lessons in their own right and to provide instructive counterpoint to the main narrative.

The truly biographical products of Johnson's career fall into two phases: the early biographies, works of the Grub Street years, the *Gentleman's Magazine* years of the late 1730s and early 1740s, which Walter Jackson Bate claims were written "partly as a form of recreation";[4] and the *Lives of the Poets*, which Johnson began in 1777 and completed in 1781. The early lives consist of eight short pieces Johnson wrote over a four-year period for the *Gentleman's Magazine*, at least a dozen sketches of physicians for Robert James's *Medicinal Dictionary*, and, the sole masterpiece of the group, the *Life of Savage* (1744) where Johnson combines several forms—personal narrative, detective story, "rogue" biography, moral essay, and literary criticism—into a complex analysis of the interplay of character strengths and weaknesses. With the exception of *Savage* (included in the *Lives of the Poets* nearly forty years later), the early biographies, which rely perhaps too heavily on their sources, draw scholarly interest primarily for displaying Johnson's wide range of intellectual interests: medicine, science, and history, as well as literature.

If, as Bate says, Johnson, with the *Life of Savage*, "invented critical biography,"[5] he advanced the mode considerably with the fifty-two biographies we know as the *Lives of the Poets*. *Savage*, perhaps, is the work where Johnson comes closest to attaining an ideal he set in *Rambler* 60 for the biographer. "The business of the biographer is often to pass slightly over those performances and incidents, which produce vulgar greatness, to lead the thoughts into domestick privacies, and display the minute details of daily life, where exterior appendages are cast aside, and men excel each other only by prudence and by virtue."[6] But, led "by the honest desire to give useful pleasure," Johnson engaged his powerful talents—his insight into the human condition, his profound moral sense, his knowledge of literary history, and his keen critical judgment—to set a uniquely Johnsonian stamp on all the "little prefaces" he had been commissioned by a cabal of London booksellers to write for a large edition of Restoration and eighteenth-century English poets. The result, of course, was a collection of lives, different in kind and scope from anything that had appeared previously.

Early in his excellent chapter devoted to Johnson's *Lives of the Poets*, Lawrence Lipking poses the question, "are the Lives admired for themselves or because there are so many ways in which they can be used?"[7] At first glance, this question seems to lead to the kind of discussion provided by Richard B. Schwartz in *Boswell's Johnson: A Preface to the Life*. Schwartz traces a twentieth-century tradition that divides biography into two generic categories, which he, for convenience, labels the "artistic" and the "scientific." While acknowledging that this distinction is "ultimately simplistic," Schwartz summarizes the basis for it: "In short, the life-writer's business is twofold: to gather facts (a quasi-scientific enterprise) and to shape facts (an artistic enterprise). The extent to which one activity is subordinate to the other will determine the type of biography which the life writer produces, either the "artistic" biography, characterized by insight, brevity, and the judicious use of key details, or the "scientific," scholarly biography which attempts to assemble every possible detail, a work in which the process of accumulation is of greater importance than the process of selection."[8]

Schwartz employs these two categories to differentiate Johnson's biographies (artistic) from Boswell's *Life of Johnson* (scientific). Recent attacks (led by Schwartz and Donald Greene) on Boswell have tended to concentrate on the alleged slipshod accumulation of data. Boswell reports hearsay and resorts to invention in a quite unscientific way; as a consequence, his "usefulness" for those seeking information about Johnson is questionable. Boswell's defenders (particularly Ralph Rader and Frederick Pottle) often argue for the biography's artistic merit.[9] With Johnson's biographies, the issue of use is somewhat different. There is little debate that as sources of information about the men whose lives he chronicled,

Johnson's biographies have long since been superseded. Their scholarly use is to provide information about Johnson, about how his mind works in the interrelationship between selection and judgment, about his views on the tradition and the particularities of English poetry, about his masterful prose style and rhetorical punch. As Ralph Rader remarks, "Johnson succeeds in his biographies because he genuinely does impose his judgment on the facts. His biographies are literature because they achieve universality of judgment. . . . The pleasure of Johnson's *Lives* is Johnson, not Pope or Addison."[10]

So the scholarly work on Johnson's biographies has tended, as Lipking's question suggests, to move in two directions: toward examining and evaluating the biographies as artistic achievements and toward mining the biographies for Johnson's interests, his ideas about morality or politics, his literary criticism.

We might classify studies of the first kind into scholarship—source studies, history of composition, etc.—and criticism—formalist analyses of structure, style, syntax, etc., and interpretations. Though much work, no doubt, remains to be done with Johnson's sources, considerable attention has been devoted to them.[11] Of note recently are Paul Hanchock's brief essay, which argues for Diogenes Laertius' *Lives of the Philosophers* (particularly the Aristotle) as a source for Johnson's tripartite structure in the major lives, and Pat Rogers's essay, which reveals Johnson's reliance on the biographical dictionaries.[12] The bulk of criticism concerning Johnson's structure focuses on one of literary biography's inherent problems, the relationship between biography and criticism, between the life of the subject and an assessment of his works. Johnson tackled this problem head on. We can recognize his awareness of the formal problem of arrangement in the full title of the work now commonly referred to as the *Lives of the Poets: Prefaces, Biographical and Critical, to the Works of the English Poets*. Johnson seems to have perceived the two functions of the "prefaces" as distinct, or at least he saw the writing task he faced as bifurcated. Most modern literary biographers, Bate or Leon Edel, for example, combine the two activities, comment-

ing on particular works when the chronological narrative ar-
rives at them. Johnson, as we know, proceeds differently: he
provides a standard chronology of the poet from pedigree to
funeral, including such details as warranted by the author's
importance and as available from Johnson's sources, and then
offers critical commentary and assessment on major works,
and an overall evaluation of the literary performance.

The second problem Johnson confronted, theoretical as well
as formal, was how to relate the author to his works. The
solution, in the major lives at least, is provided by the character section inserted between the biography and the criticism.
Johnson's writings and conversations make clear that he consistently distinguished between biography (chronological narrative) and character portraits that captured the essence of the
biographical subject. These character sections allowed
Johnson opportunities for his signal moral observations and
for attempts to account for the kinds and quality of poems on
the basis of character traits. Probably no dimension of Johnsonian biography has received more attention than these character sections, and the attention stems from several sources:
the predictable interest in them as formal connectives for
scholars examining unity and unifying principles; a fascination in them as peculiarly "Johnsonian"—the trademark moral
stance, the controversial judgments (of Milton, for example);
and an examination of them in light of theoretical debate over
the degree to which we may project into his works the biographical facts or psychological analysis of a writer. Though
Johnson is suspicious (a suspicion expressed in *Rambler* 14, for
example) of approaching a literary work through its author (or
vice versa), the nature of the relationship intrigues him; he
discusses the subject frequently, and it supplies a common
motif in his biographies—in *Savage, Prior,* and *Pope,* for example. Perhaps most interesting for Johnson is the Jekyll-and-
Hyde Milton, domestic tyrant and sublime poet, participant in
regicide and voice of Christian morality.[13]

Studies of the second kind—of Johnson and his time—cover
a predictably more varied range of subjects, from the place of
Johnsonian biography in the history of biography to Johnson's

sense of history to Johnson's critical pronouncements. In books like Jean Hagstrum's *Samuel Johnson's Literary Criticism* (1952), Leopold Damrosch Jr.'s *The Uses of Johnson's Criticism* (1976), John Vance's *Samuel Johnson and the Sense of History* (1984), Donald Greene's *The Politics of Samuel Johnson* (1963), and Paul Alkon's *Samuel Johnson and Moral Discipline* (1967), to name just a few, the authors all make extensive use of Johnson's biographies, particularly the *Lives of the Poets*, to provide the data from which to draw their conclusions. Johnson's life writings are used the same way the periodical essays, the diaries, and the sermons are used, as doors into Johnson's mind and ideas.

What, then, is the value of Johnson's biographies? One value is historical: they are, like *Tom Jones* or *Ulysses*, monuments in the history of their form. In the history of criticism or of seventeenth- and eighteenth-century poetry they provide starting places for critics and scholars, particularly those disposed to historical approaches or reception theory. Like Reynolds's *Discourses*, they stand as masterworks of that line of thought we once confidently called neoclassicism. Equally valuable is what they have to tell us about Johnson. The answer to Lipking's question posed above, then, an answer that emerges clearly in the essays that follow, is that we can both appreciate Johnson's lives as literature and use them to reveal sources of Johnson's thought. In these two intellectual endeavors, we come to "know" Samuel Johnson, both as a man and as an author, more accurately perhaps than we can know him through the Johnson handed down by legend.

In the second essay in this collection, "Life, Art, and the *Lives of the Poets*," James Battersby presents an extensive overview of many of the issues we have been considering: discovering structures and principles of connection, relating literary lives to literary works, deducing character from writings or evaluating works on the basis of character. In considering the extrapoetic personalities of the poets, Johnson is concerned with "the social, moral, and political proclivities of their works"—a peculiarly Johnsonian procedure. Battersby notes that "as we read the *Lives*, we are engaged, as we are in no other biography to a comparable degree, as much with the biographer as with his subjects." And to understand precisely the workings of this biographer, Battersby employs insightfully Wayne Booth's categories of author—real, dramatized, implied, and career—illustrating and confirming what most of us feel when reading Johnson, that "we read the *Lives* in the way that Johnson reads the poetry of his poet, with a sense of the man behind the work."

Calling upon the ideas set forth in *Rambler* 166, John Dussinger in "Dr. Johnson's Solemn Response to Beneficence" examines the curious *Life of Savage* as an exposé of the plight of the poor and the socially underprivileged in the Walpole-made world of credit and debit. Placing Savage in this socioeconomic context, Dussinger reveals a victim of a "vicious cycle of gift and obligation that results in thraldom and hatred," for whom "noble pride," a form of self-love, provides a necessary defense. Savage's well-known act of dividing his last guinea with the woman who had perjured herself against him in the murder trial provides one of the few moments in which Savage can extricate himself from external circumstances and exhibit his true virtue. This is a new angle from which to view *Savage* and one, I think, that helps account for the strange moral fiber of the work.

Johnson's intention of writing a biography or play about the warrior-king Charles XII of Sweden was recorded in 1742, about the same time he was working on *Savage* and the early *Gentleman's Magazine* biographies. Though references to Charles exist throughout Johnson's writings and recorded conversations, his is a life to which Johnson never devoted his full attention. James Gray in "Johnson's Portraits of Charles XII of Sweden" explores those qualities of the "Northern Brute" that interested Johnson, both impressing and repelling him. Gray explains the thirty-two lines of *The Vanity of Human Wishes* devoted to Charles by investigating the facts of Charles's life and speculates about Johnson's abandonment of the longer project.

Starting with the oxymoronic phrase "pleasing captivity"

extracted from the *Life of Dryden*, Catherine Parke, in her comprehensive "Johnson, Imlac, and Biographical Thinking," pursues the nature of communication between individuals that places them in the ongoingness of history connecting past, present, and future. As she examines the dynamics of discourse, Parke discusses the epistemology of learning in *Rasselas*, of literary criticism in the *Lives of the Poets*, and of history in *A Journey to the Western Islands of Scotland*.

Readers of the *Life of Milton* have long felt that Johnson treats the poet unfairly and that his particular strictures upon the poetry result from critical blind spots. Claiming that Johnson's attacks on Milton are almost exclusively on political grounds, Stephen Fix, in his "The Contexts and Motives of Johnson's *Life of Milton*," argues that Johnson attempts not to lower esteem for Milton but to strengthen his reputation by building it on firmer ground. As a consequence, Fix finds Johnson's apparent antagonism in the biography directed as much toward his predecessors in criticism and biography—the large band of Milton zealots active in the mid and late eighteenth century—as toward Milton himself. Fix employs a gardening metaphor (one that Johnson himself would have admired) to explain how Johnson prunes excessive praise that actually chokes off avenues of proper evaluation and cheapens the poet's worth in order to allow Milton's legitimate stature to achieve its proper height. Thus Johnson is not subjectively deprecating Milton's poetry but clearing away debris to make objective appraisal possible.

William Siebenschuh's "Johnson's *Lives* and Modern Students," primarily a pedagogical piece, provides a departure (or respite) from the other, critical, essays in this collection. Finding the time ripe for reintroducing Johnson into the curricula of college survey courses, both because a nostalgia for absolutes currently prevails and because his prolonged absence from such courses makes it possible for today's students to approach Johnson unencumbered by the biases that burdened past generations, Siebenschuh argues for the *Lives of the Poets* as a particularly rewarding choice of texts. Siebenschuh goes further and provides a teaching methodology, one that urges teachers to emphasize Johnson's mind in action (rather than Johnson's "historical importance")—his methods of analysis and his extraordinary ability to generalize—and to study Johnson's critical assumptions on their own terms, as starting points to stimulate student thought. "When we invite students to study Johnson, we are not asking them to study what he thought; we are inviting them to learn about thinking."

Michael Stuprich's "Johnson and Biography: Recent Critical Directions" surveys and evaluates the most significant scholarship of the past decade and a half (since the Clifford and Greene bibliography). Meant to complement the more inclusive bibliography which follows it, Stuprich's essay traces emphases and trends in existing work and suggests areas where more studies are needed.

We turn now to the first essay in the collection, Lawrence Lipking's "Johnson's Beginnings," an essay which at first glance might seem misplaced, out of step with its fellows. Did Johnson, after all, begin as a biographer? Only, I suppose, if one considers Johnson's "beginnings" as a first chapter of a life he was preparing of and for himself. But Lipking identifies, from a close reading of Johnson's early poem *On a Daffodil*, two phenomena present even in this early stage of Johnson's career—his tremendous ambition combined with a preemptive dejection: an alternation of hope and discouragement. It is just such an odd sort of combination that Johnson frequently uncovers in his studies of other writers—those remarkable insights that make Johnson's better biographies so valuable as jumping-off places for further inquiry. Lipking continues to address one of the fundamental questions facing the young Johnson: What, in the mid-eighteenth century, was left for him to do? Singling out Addison as Johnson's great precursor, Lipking defines Johnson's great project as fashioning "a prose that would wake readers up" and locates Johnson's "work of initiation" in the *Rambler*. Surely, the *Lives of the Poets* can serve as a culmination of this project.

Johnson's practice of repeating accepted truths and then questioning them, undercutting them, is also considered by Lipking, who sees the problem of authorship for Johnson as one of trying "to reach an audience already acquainted with the broad lines of truth, and already civilized by correct standards of art, and somehow, without departing from that truth and those standards, to delight it with an impression of something new."

This, it seems to me, is part of the accomplishment of the *Lives*. Johnson takes accepted truths about poets' lives, poets' works, the nature of criticism, and imparts something new, something essentially Johnsonian. Through this procedure of constantly testing truth, a procedure he also employs in the *Preface to Shakespeare*, Johnson raises the standards for biography, for literary criticism, for poetry, for the way lives should be lived. And it is Johnson's consistently high standards that render his biographies memorable, and useful, for all who read them, for all time.

LAWRENCE LIPKING

Johnson's Beginnings

The earliest surviving work by Johnson is a poem, written probably at fifteen, *On a Daffodil, the First Flower the Author Had Seen That Year*. Critics have noted the influence of Herrick and amusing anticipation of Wordsworth. But they have not remarked, I think, what makes these lines interesting. *On a Daffodil* is not only a beginner's poem but a poem about beginning: the beginning of a flower, a season of life, a career.

> Hail lovely flower, first honour of the year!
>   Hail beautious earnest of approaching spring!
> Whose early buds unusual glories wear,
>   And of a fruitfull year fair omens bring.
>
> Be thou the favorite of the indulgent sky,
>   Nor feel the inclemencies of wintry air;
> May no rude blasts thy sacred bloom destroy;
>   May storms howl gently o'er and learn to spare.

The author goes on to entreat still greater indulgence, the smiles of such beauteous virgins as divine Cleora, whose influence might fill "ev'ry fading leaf" with new verdure. But then the poem takes a sudden turn.

> But while I sing, the nimble moments fly,
>   See! Sol's bright chariot seeks the western main,
> And ah! behold the shriveling blossoms die,
>   So late admir'd and prais'd, alas! in vain!
>
> With grief this emblem of mankind I see,
>   Like one awaken'd from a pleasing dream,
> Cleora's self, fair flower, shall fade like thee,
>   Alike must fall the poet and his theme.

The sentiment is of course conventional. Yet it is also rather shocking in its hasty refusal of promise. Young Johnson does not even pause for the usual carpe diem. Committing violence against nature, he kills off the daffodil at the first nightfall, collapsing the whole season into the time it takes him to write the poem. The effect seems both self-conscious and willful. It is as if the poet had lost confidence in his verses before he came to the end, and thus slumped into an emblem that would let us know he was falling. Cleora will not smile on him, nor will he pretend that he expects to be smiled at. At the onset of spring this posy invokes a chill. Where can we go from here?

Any analysis of Johnson's beginnings as an author must take account of two phenomena, related yet oddly contradictory. The first is his tremendous ambition. In a Latin exercise composed about the same time as *On a Daffodil* and only recently printed, the young schoolboy responds to his Juvenalian theme by arguing that virtue thrives on fame and that great talents deserve great rewards. "An unsubdued and invincible desire of honour and praise is planted in our hearts, which I would believe wise Nature (for she does nothing in vain) has instilled in us to spur us to praiseworthy deeds."[1] Whether or not all hearts feel that desire, Johnson's certainly did. The evidence is too familiar to need citing here; but consider, in the poem about the daffodil, the author's almost ludicrous heaping of trophies on the poor little flower. It is the first "honour of the year" whose buds wear "unusual glories" and bring "fair omens"; it ought to be the "favorite" of the sky, a "sacred" bloom "impearl'd" with dew and bowed to like a deity, "admir'd and prais'd." All this honor and praise might be thought wasted on a daffodil, but surely some young person hungers after them. Johnson's first writing already aspires to glory.

The second phenomenon, bending back against the first and darkening it with irony, is a sort of preemptive dejection. The poet and his theme must fall; the young author will soon welcome oblivion; the scholar's life will be assailed by ills. Human wishes are vain, and the wishes of authors seem most pathetic of all. The older Johnson suggests that he learned this through experience, but young Johnson seems to have known it before a trial. He cannot look at a daffodil without seeing it shriveled. Hence the lust for glory tends to call down immediate retribution, without so much as a middle stage of temporary success. Johnson is not particularly gifted at middles; he springs directly from hope to crushing defeat. Bacon's mansion *will* fall on the head of the young enthusiast, though not for the reason he imagines. It is simply the fate of every young dreamer. This inexorable downfall of ambition is not without its problems for Johnson's work. In *Rasselas*, for instance, the preemptive dejection tends to take effect so fast that a reader has no time to entertain hope; each flower is nipped in the bud. Notoriously the book, though written to instruct the young, touches the old instead, the sadder but wiser crowd. What sort of young person could profit, at starting out, by being told that he or she should not expect to get anywhere? Only a person like Johnson.

The alliance of ambition and dejection is where Johnson begins. What explains this odd combination? It is tempting to offer a psychological cause, to stamp these proclivities with a phrase like melancholy or manic-depressive or schizophrenia or repetition compulsion or anal-erotic guilt. Psychologizing Johnson has always been a popular sport, and *On a Daffodil* might prove more interesting to a psychoanalyst than to a literary critic. Johnson himself, with his usual critical acuteness, is said to have "never much lik'd" the poem "as it was not characteristick of the Flower."[2] But in one respect the verses *are* characteristic. Botanically, the formal name of the daffodil is *Narcissus pseudo-narcissus*; and Johnson's poem reflects a classic narcissistic pattern. Its rapture over an idolized image of the self inevitably tumbles into disillusionment if not a mock suicide. In its rise and sudden fall, the flower enacts a standard male sexual fantasy, the arc of Phaethon as well as of Narcissus. Ambition ends in the bell jar or bell droop of the blossom as it leans back toward the nothingness of unsatisfied desire. Aspiring fifteen-year-old poets tend to be well acquainted with the psychology of the narcissus.

Putting aside this temptation, an interpreter might next be tempted to explain Johnson's beginnings by stressing their roots in traditional wisdom. To idolize a daffodil or a Cleora is, in fact, a mistake, as any orthodox Christian or poet would know. Those idols fade; we need to stake our hopes on higher things. Johnson's warning here may be precocious or abrupt, but that does not make it less true. At worst he is stating a truism; at best, discovering wisdom. In an eloquent analysis of *The Young Author*, Walter Jackson Bate points to the value of the recognition that dreams may come to nothing. "For the moment Johnson is simply trying to drive into himself the realization of it as a fact of human existence that must be courageously and honestly faced, and assimilated as a necessary part of living. . . . He did not need others to puncture his illusions about himself. He could do this on his own without any help."[3] This is what might be called the Mithridatic view of preemptive dejection: a little poison builds up one's resistance. Whether it worked that way for Johnson, however, may be doubted. Thinking too much about future failure can keep a young author from seizing either the day or Cleora. Daffodils need some sun. At any rate, there is something peculiar about Johnson's alternation of hope and discouragement that cannot be fully explained by traditional wisdom. Other authors, no less orthodox, wrote more encouraging fables; and Johnson's own contemporaries were struck by the strain of fatalism in his early work. His ambitions were so high, his expectations so low, that even in retrospect it is hard to see how he could begin as an author. He almost did not.

What other explanation of Johnson's beginnings can be offered? There is one sort that in my view has not been tried often enough. When psychology and wisdom have done their work, the literary critic and literary historian are still left with the basic question about a young author: What was his project? What did he think remained, in his time, for an author to do? Most Johnsonians have been strangely quiet on this subject. Even Bate, who as much as anyone else has taught us to ask the question, tends to be rather diffident about venturing an answer. Thus Johnson occupies an anomalous place in literary history, as if he gave the age its name but were somehow not part of it—a stranger in time, a generation of one. He seems to have sprung full-blown from the head of Minerva; or, to use a less heady phrase, he seems never to have made a choice of life at all, but simply to have accepted one task after another, decade by decade, like a dutiful hack (to borrow Housman's words, he "saved the sum of things for pay"). There is some truth to this view. Hawkins marveled at Johnson's want of "the impulse of genius," by which he meant that Johnson never wrote anything except under pressure and for money. Yet even a hack may be a hack of genius; and the work of genius never seems, in retrospect, to have been adventitious. In some way Johnson did choose his life as an author. But what did he choose?

The question may be clarified by considering Johnson's relation to his precursor. The identity of that precursor was well known in the eighteenth century and dominates early criticism of Johnson, though modern Johnsonians seem reluctant to bring it up. I am referring, of course, to Joseph Addison. Few literary genealogies have ever been more clearly marked or more legitimate. Addison, like Johnson, had attended the Lichfield Grammar School and, on Johnson's own account, left a reputation well suited to a schoolboy hero, since he had "planned and conducted" a *barring-out*, in which the master was locked out of his school. Johnson's longest juvenile poem is a translation of Addison's Latin *Battle of the Pygmies and Cranes*; and in the *Lives of the Poets* he later praises Roscommon as "perhaps the only correct writer in verse before Addison." *Irene*, on which Johnson expended more effort, perhaps, than on anything else he ever wrote, has always been recognized as an offspring of *Cato*. Addison's allegorical *Visions of Mirzah* is by far the most important contemporary source for all Johnson's fiction, from *The Vision of Theodore* to *Rasselas*. As the logical choice to compile the first standard English dictionary, Addison is supposed to have been offered three thousand pounds by Tonson and actually to have begun the work. Johnson defended Addison's literary criticism for awakening inquiry and expanding comprehension: "he founds art on the base of nature, and draws the principles of invention from dispositions inherent in the mind of man" (not a bad description of Johnson's own critical ideal). Most important of all, as *"the Raphael of Essay Writers"*[4] Addison had set the standard that Johnson's greatest work, the *Rambler*, deliberately set out to match. And one more point may be added: Addison's merit had been rewarded with the high post of secretary of state. In that respect, at least, Johnson never succeeded in living up to the model he had chosen.

Yet Addison had also left something to do. Despite his elegance and correctness, he had not been energetic; he had not been profound. Though young Johnson exercised his wit on the Pygmies and Cranes, the older Johnson was not sure that pygmies were worth treating in the first place. "By the sonorous magnificence of Roman syllables the writer conceals penury of thought and want of novelty, often from the reader, and often from himself."[5] Mrs. Thrale observes that while Johnson always highly commended Addison's prose, "his praises resembled those of a man who extols the superior elegance of high painted porcelain, while he himself always chuses to eat off *plate*."[6]

Hence English prose awaited a new sort of master. Johnson prided himself on refining the language by giving it weight and strength. Technically, one might describe this project in three overlapping ways. First, it is possible to stress, as W.K. Wimsatt does, the use of philosophic words. "When common words were less pleasing to the ear, or less distinct in their signification," Johnson writes, "I have familiarized the terms of philosophy by applying them to popular ideas."[7] Here, for the first time in English, the vocabulary of science turns inward, to the analysis of states of mind. Admirers praise this as a giant stride; others accuse the author of wearing stilts. Second, one might regard Johnson's project as converting the achievements of the golden age of the heroic couplet, its precise discriminations, antitheses, and balances, into the more solid medium of English prose. "Something, perhaps, I have added to the elegance of its construction, and something to the harmony of its cadence." Nadezhda Mandelstam preserved the great poems of her husband in her head; for a long time her memory was the only surviving edition. As a result of living with those rhythms and images, so intimate and familiar, she developed her own beautiful new Russian prose style, unmatched in our time. Johnson's fabulous memory may be said to have brought about a similar transformation. He carried the English poets of the late seventeenth and early eighteenth centuries in his head, and turned them into choruses of prose.

Most of Johnson's contemporaries and successors, however, would have described his prose in a third way, as reaching after "splendor and magnificence" (Robert Burrowes). Coleridge, a witness for the prosecution, charged that Johnson "creates an impression of cleverness by never saying any thing in a common way."[8] On the positive side, we may cite Johnson's own defense of a passage from the *Journey to the Western Islands*, "We were now treading that illustrious region": "the word *illustrious*, contributes nothing to the mere narration; for the fact might be told without it: but it is not, therefore, superfluous; for it wakes the mind to peculiar attention, where something of more than usual importance is to be presented. 'Illustrious!'—for what? and then the sentence proceeds to expand the circumstances connected with Iona."[9] The attack and defense agree on the effort of the prose to wake peculiar attention. Addison's elegant and correct style seldom calls attention to itself, but neither does it force one to take notice. "Against that inattention by which known truths are suffered to lie neglected," as Johnson said of Swift's prose, "it makes no provision; it instructs, but does not persuade."[10] Here was a project for the mid century: to fashion a prose that would wake readers up. At this Johnson certainly succeeded. Though some

readers were extremely irritated at being wakened or shaken
so roughly (by "bow-wow sounds" like a barking dog in the
night), most readers, like Nathan Drake, applauded the effects
of the heightened new style: "to clothe with fresh energy the
maxims of virtue and of piety, perhaps unparalleled in the
powers of impression."[11] Addison was displaced. Johnson's
prose, somewhat adulterated with sugar and water, became
the standard prose of Victorian England.

Yet the project had its dangers, as Johnson knew. What he
most admired Addison for was not his prose but its consistent
employment in the service of truth. "All the enchantment of
fancy and all the cogency of argument are employed to recommend to the reader his real interest, the care of pleasing the
Author of his being."[12] Hence Johnson's advice to James Woodhouse, the shoemaker poet: "Give nights and days, Sir, to the
study of Addison, if you mean either to be a good writer, or
what is more worth, an honest man."[13] The last clause is
crucial. Johnson thought nothing more important than train-
ing his readers to be good, according to the unchallengeable
dictates of revelation. "I shall never envy the honours which
wit and learning obtain in any other cause, if I can be num-
bered among the writers who have given ardour to virtue, and
confidence to truth." Addison deserved the highest praise as a
teacher of wisdom, one who had published nothing that he
would have to regret in his last moments. That was Johnson's
ambition too. His project demanded not only that his writing
be useful, but that it be *perfect*. Not many ambitious young
authors can ever have faced so stringent and fearful a task.

No wonder that he found it so hard to begin. He was still
beginning, in fact, well into his forties. A recent critic has
argued that most great authors produce a work of initiation,
which not only achieves the essential breakthrough but also
explains its principles, teaching us how to read it. In these
terms Johnson's initiation is the *Rambler*. It begins with no
fewer than five essays that discuss the problems of beginning,
weigh the alternatives, and define the project. The first is the
well-known paper on "the difficulty of the first address on any
new occasion," which explains the advantages of writing short

papers without any larger commitment. The second defends the human tendency to embark on great enterprises while dreaming of future rewards, although "perhaps no class of the human species requires more to be cautioned against this anticipation of happiness, than those that aspire to the name of authors." The third considers the difficult "task of an author" by means of an allegory on Criticism, which tends "to hinder the reception of every work of learning or genius." The fourth is the famous essay on modern fiction, which in this context and the context of Johnson's own fiction may be viewed as an internal debate about whether the novel is a proper medium for representing life, since almost inevitably novelists "confound the colours of right and wrong" by mixing virtue with vice. The fifth, like *On a Daffodil*, is about "the spring of the year, and the spring of life"; addressing young readers, the Rambler warns them "that a blighted spring makes a barren year, and that the vernal flowers, however beautiful and gay, are only intended by nature as preparatives to autumnal fruits." Is Johnson regretting some blight of his own, or harvesting personal fruit? Ambitious, or dejected? Perhaps the issue was still not settled for him.

The problem of beginning as Johnson sees it may be illuminated by one of his most interesting disagreements with Addison, the discussion, in *Rambler* 158, of how a poem should begin. Addison thinks that the answer is easy: the first lines ought to be "plain, simple, and unadorned,"[14] as in the ancient epics or *Paradise Lost*. But Johnson points out the flaw in both the precept and the examples. In fact great poems open with plenty of glitter. Beginning requires a special effort, both to catch the reader and to show the author's power.

> The intent of the introduction is to raise expectation, and suspend it; something therefore must be discovered, and something concealed; and the poet, while the fertility of his invention is yet unknown, may properly recommend himself by the grace of his language.
>
> He that reveals too much, or promises too little; he that never irritates the intellectual appetite, or that imme-

diately satiates it, equally defeats his own purpose. It is necessary to the pleasure of the reader, that the events should not be anticipated, and how then can his attention be invited, but by grandeur of expression?

There is material here for a whole treatise on beginnings. But a few points seem particularly relevant to Johnson's own career. First, the issue between the Spectator and the Rambler is exactly the same as the difference that contemporaries observed between the styles of Addison and Johnson: on the one hand, a mode "plain, simple, and unadorned," whose elegance sometimes verges on insipidity; on the other, a "grandeur of expression" loaded on the subject, not always appropriately. Significantly, each critic perceives Milton as an illustration of his own principles. For Addison, he is striking because of the directness with which he manages his plot; for Johnson, because of his sublime grandeur of expression—"Milton's style was not modified by his subject." As much as Johnson respects the truth, he does not think that a writer will succeed by revealing it all at the beginning. Some glitter must first catch the eye.

The second point is Johnson's recommendation of temporary concealment, in order to *suspend* expectation as well as raise it. The audience must be left hanging. Such suspension follows an aesthetic principle, of course, the need to please the reader by inducing that faintly anxious attention that we call suspense. But it also bears on the author's own problem at beginning, his need to show his power or "recommend himself." An ambitious author like Johnson, proud of his abilities yet conscious that his success will depend on attracting or catering to others, may well be torn between two approaches: defiance and seduction. It may be best for him to suspend the choice. The first number of the *Rambler* is a fascinating study of this state of mind. "If a man could glide imperceptibly into the favour of the publick, and only proclaim his pretensions to literary honours when he is sure of not being rejected," the yet unknown Johnson says, "he might commence author with better hopes." Yet since authors are known to be both ambitious and vulnerable, it is no wonder that some "should endeavour to gain favour by bribing the judge with an appearance of respect which they do not feel," and others should try to attract regard "by a daring profession of their own deserts, and a publick challenge of honours and rewards." This is no mere theoretical question. The Rambler is obviously talking about himself, and Johnson's beginning hangs in the balance. He solves the problem only by letting it hang. "But whether my expectations are most fixed on pardon or praise, I think it not necessary to discover; for having accurately weighed the reasons for arrogance and submission, I find them so nearly equiponderant, that my impatience to try the event of my first performance will not suffer me to attend any longer the trepidations of the balance." Once again he *suspends* expectation. Arrogance and submission must be equally concealed, or answered by the event. Johnson did not resolve his opposing inclinations toward ambition and dejection. Instead he put them both to use and based his work on the conflict. That is how he managed to begin.

The conflict hangs over Johnson's own most literal beginnings, his weighty opening sentences. "It is a truth universally acknowledged. . . ." Whatever truth follows, the reader eventually learns, will turn out to be not quite true. Our first impression and judgment must be suspended. The energy of Johnson's analysis is supplied by his skepticism, his determination to examine every received opinion and find something wanting. It is no accident that the Rambler chose as his motto Horace's famous boast, *Nullius addictus jurare in verba magistri* (Not bound to swear to the words of any master). Johnson is his own man, and the simultaneous assertion and qualification of certified "truth" is his special signature. Even the most ambitious generalization must suffer a fall. It may be instructive to contrast this habit of mind with one that, on the surface, seems identical to the point of parody. "It is a truth universally acknowledged, that a single man in possession of a good fortune, must be in want of a wife." Jane Austen was a fine

Johnsonian, and her play on the formula follows the master not only in its lofty "truth" but in its clever unsettling of expectations. We might even credit her with recreating not only Johnson's formal text but his secret motive, a challenge to the "universally acknowledged." But in one respect her sentence is not like one of Johnson's: While seeming to satirize her opening proposition, she actually believes it. The whole of *Pride and Prejudice* tells us that; all wealthy single men do end up taking wives. The author may think that received opinion is comical, but she does not think it false. Johnson is far more subversive. He states the opening truth so seriously, so philosophically, that we are always tempted to accept it. But Johnson is smarter than we are, and knows better. The seeming truth covers a crack, perhaps an abyss. He opens up his text by delving there.

One final word about the implications of such beginnings for Johnson's project. If my analysis is at all persuasive, then the bending back of Johnson's work against itself, the preemption built into his ambition, ought to seem not merely a matter of psychology or convention but a strategy for dealing with the problem of authorship in his time. That problem, as he sees it, is to reach an audience already acquainted with the broad lines of truth, and already civilized by correct standards of art, and somehow, without departing from that truth and those standards, to delight it with an impression of something new. His whole generation shared the dilemma; though Johnson thought that many in his generation had evaded rather than solved it, by chasing after untruth and incorrectness. His own solution was different. He would raise the standards higher by being satisfied with nothing less than perfection and by bringing life itself to the test of truth. He would of course fail. That failure is built into Johnson's beginnings, his discontent with the half-truths of writing even as he writes them down. Disillusionment shadows Johnson's illusions from the moment of their making; at fifteen, he already cannot wait for the daffodil to bloom before he blasts it. Yet that too is a way to begin. The same great expectations and self-conscious doubts that made it so hard for Johnson to start would eventually prove the means of his deliverance, the talents he was born to employ. He projected his life as a writer from such beginnings. The problems he found there would follow him to the end.

JAMES L. BATTERSBY

Life, Art, and the
Lives of the Poets

In a recent discussion of the enduring popularity of biographical literature, Denis Donoghue has suggested that biography is "the genre most congenial to an unassertive humanism," the one that from its inception to its latest incarnation is unashamedly attached to a "vocabulary of selfhood, identity, personality, individuality," as well as to all those notions implicated in its foundational terms (independent action, choice, will, etc.), and depends on and assumes an "unembarrassed sense of character."[1] With the concepts, if not with the terms, of this vocabulary, Johnson, of course, would be comfortable, and perhaps no biographer has exhibited a greater capacity than he to delineate character, if by "character" we mean the expression of "the sum of the moral and mental qualities which distinguish an individual or a race," "the individuality impressed by nature and habit,"[2] or, as Johnson himself says in the *Dictionary*, "personal constitution of the mind," "that which distinguishes any thing or person from others." And perhaps it is fair to say that no one has had a better sense than Johnson of what constitutes excellence in biography. From *Rambler* 60 and his scattered remarks elsewhere—in the periodical papers, in the *Lives of the Poets*, in Boswell's *Life of Johnson* and *Tour to the Hebrides*—the reader can recover the durable principles of the art of life writing; and in Johnson's practice as a biographer, he can witness the immanent projection of virtually all the qualities that in the eyes of at least one modern commentator distinguish "first-rate biography: ceaseless quest for the essence of the subject's character, the application of the biographer's experience of the world to the moral and psychological problems his narrative raises, the spirit of skepticism governed by common sense."[3]

Yet the same commentator who finds in Johnson the local habitation and name of biographical excellence is also obliged to conclude that "he showed his age what a biography should contain; he did not demonstrate how it should be built." That is, the reader finds in the *Lives* "a miscellany of facts rather than . . . coherent portraits" and looks in vain for "formal structure" or "structural logic." Johnson "moved restlessly from point to point . . . [and] hung his data together in chronological sequence, without any nice proportioning of part to part."[4]

For the moment, I shall defer any consideration of the appropriateness of these judgments and note only that if they were accurate, we could say in Johnson's behalf what he said to Reynolds in reference to the *Dictionary*, that he could state how a biography should be executed in the most perfect manner and then show from various causes why the execution had not been equal to what the author promised to himself.[5] Moreover, if we put the matter of structural coherence aside temporarily, we can immediately explain certain obvious weaknesses in Johnson's accounts of the poets by appealing to the paucity of his information. Johnson had access to many works but to few significant particulars relating to the progress of the poets through life, to their conduct and behavior over time. Speaking of the difficulties he encountered in his efforts to accumulate details that would enrich, indeed, make possible, an account of Pater, Denis Donoghue rehearses Johnson's condition relative to almost all the poets whose lives he was under contract to illuminate: "if a biography needs events as the composition of bricks needs straw, Pater's biographer is nearly straw-less."[6] Over and over again, Johnson informs us that he has neither straw nor clay sufficient to his task ("Of Sir John Denham very little is known"; of Butler little is known and "more . . . cannot now be learned"; etc.),[7] and, in the middle of his labors, he informs Mrs. Thrale that she is "at all places of high resort . . . while [he is] seeking for something to say about men of whom [he knows] nothing but their verses and sometimes little of them."[8] Even of poets of whom his knowledge was unusually rich, he had few details that were useful for purposes of discrimination. For example, "From any minute knowledge of [Addison's] familiar manners, the intervention of sixty years has now debarred us." Indeed, to read the *Lives* through, with attention focused on resonant biographical facts, on data capable of betraying characteristic behavior, is to be struck by how much more we have of heath than vegetable exuberance, of the rocks of Scotland than the bustle of the Strand. As a biographer, Johnson had least of what he most desired, knowledge of "those minute peculiarities which discriminate every man from all others" (*Life of Browne*).

On the other hand, it must be admitted that assiduity was not his strong suit. Although he made considerable efforts to enlarge his store of details, consulting printed records and memorial testimony and petitioning friends and acquaintances to undertake some of the lives, especially when they could be supposed to have access to hereditary or privileged information (Lord Westcote and Dr. Farmer, for example), honesty extorts from partiality the observation that, like Dryden, Johnson was "no lover of labor" and did not always add sedulous inquiry to his other burdens. Moreover, although Johnson sometimes included less than he knew (choosing, for example, from available anecdotes in Spence's collection those that correlated positively with his controlling conception of the peculiar genius of, say, Pope or Addison),[9] he often inserted material only because he had it (Dryden's summer and winter seats, for example). And the extreme brevity of some lives, the unmistakable signs of expedition and hurry in others, indicate that Johnson wrote, as he said, "dilatorily and hastily, unwilling to work and working with vigour and haste."[10] To all this we can add that in preparing to write Johnson spent little time reviewing the works of the poets,[11] depending more confidently on memory than a scholar beseems.

Clearly, if we set doggedly about the task of identifying every defect in the *Lives*, whether occasioned by causes inherent in the task and materials or by shortcomings in the biographer, that highlights the disparity between what Johnson performed and what he could conceive, we could accumulate "faults sufficient to obscure and overwhelm any other merit,"[12] except those merits, of course, that have yet to be discussed but that insure that the work will remain one of the lasting monuments of our culture. Indeed, such a list, however extensive, would only show how much Johnson could give away without losing our esteem for his achievement. To alter Johnson's remarks about Shakespeare slightly, we can obviously say that if the *Lives* has many faults, it likewise has many excellencies.

So far, I have said little about criticism, but certainly the *Lives* is, as Bate says, not only "a classic of world literature," but "a landmark in the history of criticism."[13] What we have are not "little Lives, and little Prefaces, to a little edition of the English Poets," but, rather, extraordinarily rich *Prefaces, Biographical and Critical, to the Works of the English Poets,* a collection of pieces in which both criticism and biography achieve eminence and, in my view, combine in a variety of ways. It is to the relation between the two that I would now like to turn, giving particular attention to what may be embedded in Lawrence Lipking's suggestive notion that in the *Lives* we have "literary criticism based on a criticism of life."[14]

Johnson knew not how it could be proved that if Dryden had written less he would have written better. Similarly, I know not how it could be proved that if Johnson had written with more pertinent particulars at his command or arranged his materials differently he would have written better. What we know with certainty is that the *Lives* stands alone; there is nothing in previous or subsequent literature comparable to the *Lives*. The achievement, even as a kind, depends very immediately on the peculiar abilities, knowledge, and experience of Johnson. To emulate Johnson's achievement, the biographer would need not only to find in himself something answerable to the stretch and reach of Johnson's mind, the range of his learning, and the breadth of his comprehension, but also to adopt the principles, both moral and critical, that inform his practice. If he did the latter, he would also understand why, to Johnson, biography and criticism are intimately and inevitably related. To write criticism from the Johnsonian perspective is to write about humans, their powers, habits, and tendencies of mind, about the achievements of human beings as actualized records of moral and aesthetic choices, as solid embodiments of what, under the impulse of multifarious ambitions, needs, wishes, and necessities, man has been able to perform.

If we pause after reading the *Lives* through and ask ourselves what sticks in the mind, what facts, details, arguments, and so on force themselves on recollection, in all likelihood we will momentarily imitate the gaper, stare brilliantly ahead in openmouthed silence, until our attention is directed to, say, Milton, or blank verse, or the Pindaric ode, or the pastoral. With terms as trigger mechanisms, articulation becomes possible. Such prompting will bring back a surprising amount of material, perhaps more of it pertaining to judgments of poems than to judgments of persons. But if for a moment we think about what Johnson has said about poets, with special reference to those terms, categories, and concerns to which he regularly recurs, we will notice, I think, how frequently Johnson directs us, not only in the "characters" but throughout the lives, to self-confidence, to self-assurance, to the conduct and genius of the poets, to their vigor of mind, their ambition, their learning. Indeed, so pervasive is the language relating to moral and intellectual qualities, to personal endowment and habit, that, despite the dearth of "biographical" particulars and minute peculiarities of conduct, we have, finally, very rich and complex impressions of the distinctive characters of the poets, at least of those who receive extended treatment. We feel we know the men as well as the works, even though most of the relevant information about them derives from the writings. Moreover, if "it is the proper ambition of the heroes in literature to enlarge the boundaries of knowledge by discovering and conquering new regions of the intellectual world" (*Rambler* 137), and if "self-confidence is the first requisite to great undertakings" (*Lives* 3:89), then from the promontory that overlooks the whole collection, we can see many of the poets forming on one or the other side of the great intellectual fault line separating magnanimity and pusillanimity, temerity and timidity, boldness and caution, enterprise and cowardice. For example, Milton, Dryden, Pope, Otway, Savage, "Rag" Smith, and Gray are representative of those who either completed or were capable of completing bold designs, whereas Addison, Waller, Roscommon, John Philips, and Walsh are representative of those who rather adorned or refined than extended or perfected their intellectual legacy.

Like Dryden and Pope, whose minds were "always curious, always active," "ambitious," and "adventurous," Milton "had the usual concomitant of great abilities, a lofty and steady confidence in himself" (*Lives* 1:94). Perhaps one of the most striking passages in the *Lives* is the one in which Johnson, working from an achieved conception of the characteristic Milton, roams at large (not untypically) in the fields of pure, though not idle speculation, surmising Milton's probable response to the sluggish pace with which *Paradise Lost* crept upon popular esteem: "Fancy can hardly forbear to conjecture with what temper Milton surveyed the silent progress of his work, and marked his reputation stealing its way in a kind of subterraneous current through fear and silence. I cannot but conceive him calm and confident, little disappointed, not at all dejected, relying on his own merit with steady consciousness, and waiting without impatience, the vicissitudes of opinion, and the impartiality of a future generation" (*Lives* 1:144). How Milton actually responded we will never know with any certainty. Johnson gives us but one of many possibilities, but that Milton reacted as Johnson imagines he did, we have little doubt. The response is more than possible; it is plausible, given the working hypothesis of the man on which Johnson depends and which we as a consequence adopt.

The essay that deliberately and patiently explores the extent to which our conceptual grasp of character depends upon Johnson's conjectures and surmises has yet to be written, but repeatedly Johnson extrapolates from the known on the basis of what is implicated in the general nature of man or in the particular genius of the individual, his principal purpose being either to demystify the wonders that we are fond of propagating or to outline more firmly the essential lineaments of the individual. Moreover, insufficient emphasis has been given to the ways in which Johnson's overarching, controlling "image" of the poet determines the nature and range of the conjectural probabilities that specific events or circumstances are seen to entail. Life is various, and just as the same cause can produce diverse effects, so the same effect can spring from disparate causes.

> Vices and errors are differently modified, according to the state of the minds to which they are incident: to indulge hope beyond the warrant of reason, is the failure alike of mean and elevated understandings; but its foundation and its effects are totally different: the man of high courage and great abilities, is apt to place too much confidence in himself, and to expect from a vigorous exertion of his powers more than spirit or diligence can attain. . . . The drone of timidity presumes likewise to hope, but without ground and without consequence; the bliss with which he solaces his hours, he always expects from others.[15]

For example, if steady advancement to positions of increasing responsibility in the state argues for administrative competence, then both Prior and Addison would have to be judged competent; but that Johnson invokes the argument in behalf of Prior and not Addison, despite Pope's testimony against Prior, tells us, among other things, how probabilities were filtered through his different conceptions of the poets.[16] Johnson's handling of the mercurial John Gay is also instructive as an example of selective inference. Manic-depressive behavior allows for a variety of social implications not specified by

Johnson. That Gay's rapid fluctuations between hope and despondency might imply, as Johnson suggests, "a soft and civil companion" (*Lives* 2:272) can be granted persuasive probability only on the assumption of a predominant conception of Gay's basic temperament. Finally, within the space of a few short pages Johnson firmly establishes, by force of supposition from Congreve's works, what we confidently accept as true of three aspects of the writer's character: Congreve completed his preparatory studies "as may be reasonably supposed with great celerity and success" (*Lives* 2:213); "it may be . . . reasonably supposed that his manners were polite, and his conversation pleasing" (*Lives* 2:224); and in "his retirement he may be supposed to have applied himself to books" (*Lives* 2:226). When hard biographical particulars cannot be inducted into service, then conjecture must supply their place. But from the available facts and especially from the writings, Johnson creates distinct characters, to the substantial validity of which supplementary facts would, we feel, "only prove by events the reasonableness of opinions" (*Milton*). As we read, we are struck by how well-defined our impressions of the poets are; as we reflect, by how much our security depends upon conjecture.

On the side of timidity, we have several poets of whom Addison may stand as the epitome. Addison is "deliberate and cautious," he "did not trust his powers enough to be negligent," and he never deviated "from his track to snatch a grace." "He thinks justly, but he thinks faintly." These poets may refine our numbers, purify our diction, endow the known with special graces of expression, impress truth in novel and felicitous ways, but they seldom display the human reach at its stretch or force us to alter significantly our working understanding of the capacities of man. Waller has "elegance and gaiety," but he is "never pathetic" and "rarely sublime." Similarly, Walsh has "more elegance than vigour" and "seldom rises higher than to be pretty." And though Roscommon is "elegant," he is "not great"; he "improved taste, if he did not enlarge knowledge." Regularly in the *Lives*, where we find in the writing vigor, strength, and energy, more of nature and truth, more that is pathetic or sublime, we find in the poets boldness, courage, self-conscious merit—high opinion of self being more often than not a sovereign mistress of large effects. On the other hand, where we find elegance, prettiness, and felicity without ardor or vehemence in the writing, we find in the poets caution, timidity, deliberateness, even cowardice. Moreover, to illustrate and aggrandize his distinctions, Johnson repeatedly relies on a surprisingly stable stock of metaphoric vehicles, which, while notably present in the *Lives*, is nowhere seen in fuller deployment than in the *Preface to Shakespeare*, where suns blaze and satellites reflect diminished light, where indissoluble fabrics withstand the tides that destroy sand castles, where mines contain in inexhaustible plenty what precious cabinets selectively display as polished rarities, where forests are majestic and shaven lawns pretty, where oaks and cedars tower over shrubs and velvet lawns, where adventurers explore and conquer territories that others civilize and domesticate, where lions shake dewdrops from their manes and eagles fly high or stay long on the wing. To read the *Lives* with a mind alert to the often subtle ways in which Johnson exploits the categories of the metaphoric core for the purpose of exemplifying character, while keeping in mind that the contrasting, correlative item is frequently rather implied than stated, is to notice how often description is invested with normative weight.

Of course, in tracing these divisions and lines of affiliation in the *Lives*, we are emphasizing only one salient aspect of Johnson's perdurable interest in the relation between artistic production and human agency, one, however, that is centrally related to his concern with presumption and caution, a theme recurrent in the periodical papers.[17] Certainly in the individual lives Johnson shows us the gold mixed with baser matter (Milton's surly independence, Dryden's querulousness and petulance, Pope's mean stratagems and petty pride), the care as well as the happiness of writing, and the extraordinarily diverse ways in which the qualities requisite to greatness may be manifested, to either the credit or discredit of the poet's humanity. Still, this aspect of the *Lives*, especially when augmented by a familiarity with the relevant periodical papers, reminds us that Johnson is concerned, here as elsewhere, not only with distinguishing the peculiar properties of exemplary achievement and locating the bases of its possibility in human temperament, but also with activating our energies and animating our hopes. Quietly, but with eloquent persistence, Johnson encourages us to strike our flint against objects to determine whether it can produce fire; and to recognize that the complement extern of hope or desire can be realized only by activity and effort not rendered chill and lifeless by the sort of frigorific wisdom that confounds prudence and cowardice, difficulty and impossibility.

Had Johnson not been engaged to write prefaces both biographical and critical, he would perhaps have arranged his materials differently, thereby saving us the bother of trying to discover precedents for his most common division of the lives into units of biography, character, and criticism and to find some happy role of coadunation for the middle part. Had he, further, been blessed with knowledge of more telling particulars, he would undoubtedly have enriched our understanding of peculiar character in unforeseen ways. What seems certain, however, from what we know of his early lives (including *Savage*) and from the principles recoverable from his writings, is that what Keast has called the "characteristic linkage of biography and criticism"[18] would have been preserved. In *Idler* 102, Johnson noted that the "gradations of a hero's life are from battle to battle, and of an author's from book to book." And from Hagstrum and our direct perusal of Johnson's practice, we know that he looked upon writing as a performance, as a kind of activity or behavior that revealed the powers of the author. To be sure, as Hagstrum says, "He also considered the work as an expression of the reality and nature that the poet had observed and contemplated, and he was profoundly concerned with the psychological effects of the work upon its readers. But the consideration of the performance as evidence of personal endowment is at least of cognate importance with the others."[19] Johnson tells us that "to know anything . . . we must know its effects; to see men we must see their works";[20] and that "there is always a silent reference from human works to human abilities" (*Preface to Shakespeare* 81). Briefly, the author is central and preeminent in Johnson's critical scheme, because as the one responsible for the disposition in the work of the materials of nature and reality, he is the source of the pleasures effected in the reader, and because "the enquiry, how far man may extend his designs, or how high he may rate his native force, is of far greater dignity than in what rank we shall place any particular performance" (ibid.). Reasoning from the achieved effect of pleasure (or dissatisfaction) in the common reader back to the causes of that effect,[21] mediately in the details of the work, ultimately in the capacities of the author, Johnson makes the determination of the character of the poet a central element of critical inquiry. A substantial portion of Johnson's criticism is given over to a consideration of literature as the creative acts of poets endowed by nature, education, and experience with qualities of mind or character that, textually embodied, evoke responses that cannot be explained adequately by reference to the formal or technical traits of texts.

Although many readers might quibble with some elements of this capsule summary of Johnson's criticism, so far as I know no modern commentator on the *Lives* would recoil from Hagstrum's opinion that Johnson viewed a work "as a revelation of the powers of the author,"[22] or Folkenflik's that Johnson "draws inferences about his subjects from their writings."[23] What causes trouble are the clumsy and awkward attempts by some critics, fond of Johnson and hobbyhorses, to treat writing as autobiography, to establish direct correspondences between the professions of poetic speakers and the practices of historical persons, or between the traits of represented characters and those of the bipedalian creatures who stub their toes, digest food, and sometimes write. Ever since Krutch in the early forties had the temerity to assert that Johnson had not only "a passionate interest in character and manners but also a concomitant of that passionate interest—namely, a tendency to look in poetry for the character of the poet,"[24] critics have been eager to save Johnson from acting in complicity with the genetic fallacy, perhaps sometimes exhibiting a "reflex" conditioned by "new critical" arguments or fiats, but more frequently displaying a special sensitivity to the manifest complexity and sophistication of Johnson's thought. M.H. Abrams, for example, thinks that Krutch is wrong and calls what he is up to "literary physiognomy."[25] And although Hagstrum recognizes that Johnson saw poetry as revelatory of the powers of the author, he is quick to add that Johnson was not "guilty of what has been called the personal heresy. He did not expect a poet to hold the mirror up to the events of his own life or to the variegations of his own taste, nor did he examine poetry in order to reconstruct the poet's biography or to psychoanalyze his personality."[26] More recently, however, a certain tentativeness has been encroaching upon, without enfeebling, the opposition to Krutch. Lawrence Lipking, for example, seems at times to be caught between conflicting perceptions. On the one hand, he is convinced that Johnson's descriptions of the political and poetic Milton "are internally consistent" and that "from the *Life of Milton* as a whole we receive an impression of Milton that is indivisible."[27] On the other hand, he is certain that in the *Lives* "Johnson faced one insuperable problem in demonstrating the connection between a poet's life and work: he did not trust such connections. . . . A serious critic, Johnson thought, could not indulge the vulgar fallacy of confusing the personality revealed by the poet's life with the genius and powers manifested in his poems."[28] And if Leopold Damrosch finds more mediation between life and work than others, he, too, is reluctant to press the connections. According to Damrosch, Johnson is able to "concentrate on the poems, and on biography chiefly as it accounts for poems, . . . without compromising his fundamental belief that human life must be seen and judged as a whole. To be sure, a man's writings are not synonymous with his character, and good poems are not always written by good men. . . . Johnson is commendably cautious in establishing relations between poetry and biography."[29] But perhaps no one has more directly addressed the issue than Folkenflik, who devotes two chapters of his book to a discussion of how Johnson understood the relations between writings and poets.[30] In the end, however, the many correspondences between social and poetical action notwithstanding, he is obliged to acknowledge that "Johnson intentionally lays out the sections of a biography separately because the life and the work are essentially different things, though conduct and poems are products of the same human agency."[31] Thus, the resistance to Krutch persists, even as the terms of disagreement moderate.

Of course, the evidence against Krutch supplied by Johnson himself is quite impressive, taken at large. Of the many passages available for service, three are most frequently cited, none more often than the following section of the *Life of Thomson:* "The biographer of Thomson has remarked, that an author's life is best read in his works: his observation was not well-timed. Savage, who lived much with Thomson once told me, how he heard a lady remarking that she could gather from his works three parts of his character; that he was *a great Lover, a great Swimmer,* and *rigorously abstinent;* but said Savage, he knows not any love but that of the sex; he was never in cold water in his life; and he indulges himself in all the luxury that comes within his reach" (*Lives* 3:297-98). Next in order of citation is the opening of *Rambler* 14: "Among the many inconsistencies which folly produces, or infirmity suffers in the human mind, there has often been observed a manifest and striking contrariety between the life of an author and his writings."[32] And, finally, readers are usually directed to the *Life of Savage,* where the disparity between profession and practice is directly exemplified by Savage, who "mistook the love for the practice of virtue, and was indeed not so much a good man as the friend of goodness" (*Lives* 2:380). Strong evidence this, and not to be overwhelmed by mere tricks of verbal legerdemain.

In taking up the issue once more, on my way to showing how the excellencies of the *Lives* more than compensate for any actual or alleged faults in its materials or structural organization, I am not hoping to achieve eminence (or even notoriety) from the "heresies of paradox" by standing received opinion on its head and asserting that the case is just the reverse of what we always thought it was. Nor is it my aim to make Krutch either hero or goat of some critical narrative. He, like the other commentators, is not in the business of making Johnson simpleminded, is no retailer of flocculence peddling bags of wool. Whenever anyone wishes to make Johnson speak like the lady of Savage's acquaintance, or whenever anyone blithely assumes that the person who writes as a philosopher must obviously live like one, then upon such spokesmen the full thunder of Johnson's rejoinders may be released. But such advocates are rare and usually made of the same haylike substance that out of them we kick. As we have seen, virtually every modern commentator recognizes that from the writings Johnson educes powers of mind, habits, tendencies of thought, and characteristic levels or kinds of action; several also detect certain correspondences between his representations of the conduct and the literary action of poets. Clearly, although poets "do not always express their own thoughts," as Johnson says in the *Life of Pope*, they sometimes do, and even when the poet expresses something other than he believes or practices, he necessarily discloses aspects of his intellectual or poetic character, betraying not only peculiar habits and processes of thought, but also dictional preferences, analytic skills, the nature and extent of his learning, and so on. To be sure, the good writer is not *always* a good man, and Johnson was keenly aware of how easily the sound precepts of the "vicious moralist"—the man who wrote better than he lived—could lose their authority when they were found to have no impact on his own behavior. Nevertheless, Johnson also knew that writings display aspects of character that cannot be faked or falsely represented. Moral nature sometimes but intellectual nature always, like murder, will out.

Although much of this has been recognized, too many critics (including those cited above) have approached the issue of art and life with a severely restricted and reductive notion of "author." Consequently, they have not done enough to identify the nature and extent of Johnson's dependence on the writings for his understanding of the poets or to correlate the various classes of information that the writings yield with the critical framework (including the questions and categories of interest it entails) upon which he steadfastly relies. Johnson learns so much about poets from the writings because he asks certain questions (often implicitly), has certain interests, and adopts a certain procedure of reasoning from psychological effects to psychological causes. As I suggested above, Johnson's critical method is a worthy one, as valuable today as it has always been. (It is but a special example of a mode of reasoning belonging to a tradition that stretches from Longinus to Fredric Jameson and includes such critics as Addison, Pope, Coleridge, Arnold, Sainte-Beuve, Pater, and Eliot.) As employed by Johnson, it enables us to know something about the capacities of humans, about the combination of the new and the familiar in ways that produce in the reader pleasures deriving from the apprehension of truth and novelty. Johnson takes as his starting point the end of poetry, pleasing instruction, accomplished by bringing imagination to the help of reason. He then goes on to examine the causes of that pleasure, mediated by the text, in the author, separating his accidental advantages and limitations (those depending upon education, models, conventions, the state of learning, the age, and so on) from his particular ability to contribute to our understanding of the capacities of man as those have been established by a long succession of endeavors. Broadly speaking, Johnson is a qualitative critic, interested primarily, not in the technical, linguistic, or formal features of texts, but in those qualities of mind (or personality), time, and value that distinguish productions and producers. In the *Lives*, Johnson combines and conflates his interests, often taking up issues together that for purposes of analysis I will here separate into three distinct categories.

First, Johnson focuses on those details of statement (opinions, views, ideas), representation (character, fable, etc.), and expression (diction, prosody, imagery, etc.) in texts that one by one or collectively impress upon us a sense of a particular kind of mind or sensibility or a peculiar way of thinking about or arranging the experiences and values of life. It is this tendency in Johnson to move from writings to poets that most critics readily acknowledge, for everywhere in the *Lives*, most notably, of course, in the intellectual and poetic characters (but even in instances of local textual criticism), there can be found the subordination of technical and formal matters to those more general concerns that have their locus in the capacities of authors to express or excite thoughts and feelings answerable to our nature under specified conditions.[33]

The terms governing inquiry here are not genre specific or text specific, but are applicable to works of all kinds and can be identified roughly with the primary categories of Longinian analysis, i.e., *thought*, the immanent reflection of the author's characteristic way of conceiving things; *emotion*, the textually embedded projection of the author's distinctive sensibility; and *expression*, the devices of language by which the author's thought and emotion are artistically realized. Working in this mode, with these categories, requires comparative judgment, since kind and degree of qualitative achievement can be determined only by reference to other manifestations of the qualities or to some conception of the possibilities naturally inhering in the thought or emotion (comparison here being founded on broad human experience). As Johnson says, "Demonstration immediately displays its power . . . but works tentative and experimental must be estimated by their proportion to the general and collective ability of man" (*Preface to Shakespeare* 60). In things "admitting of gradation and comparison" (*Cowley*), nothing can be "stiled excellent till it has been compared with other works of the same kind" (*Preface to Shakespeare*). Throughout the *Lives*, Johnson employs the comparative method, often silently, as he pronounces judgment on the lack of nature or emotion in this or that work or author, on kinds and degrees of correctness, and so on. It is Johnson's principal mode of discussion, though its prevalence is often obscured by flat assertion, by what appears to be the magisterial ukase; i.e., the standard against which achievement is measured is implied rather than stated. Nevertheless, as we read through the *Lives*, encountering successive achievements with class affinities, we gain greater and greater confidence in

Johnson's judgments. Of all modes of criticism, this one is most susceptible to impressionism and bigoted authoritarianism. The practitioner's suasive power is directly proportionate to his broad experience and his manifest powers of discrimination and analysis. Thus, because its focus is on the sensibility and genius of writers, and because it depends for its effectiveness on our concessions to the demonstrated authority of its advocate, this mode of criticism is practiced with success by very few. (A moment of reflection on this point tells us why Johnson is one of those heroes of literature who is rather admired than imitated.)

Second, as a critic, Johnson is concerned with questions that consider the author's achievement in relation to his circumstances, to the possibilities and limitations determined by models, poverty, education, patronage, occasions, conventions, available translations, and, indeed, all those extrapoetic factors that precondition actual expression, including the temperament of the author, his readiness to attack, his pride and vanity, and his needs. What is not generally recognized, I think, is how frequently Johnson resorts to writings to establish not only the literary qualities and traditions the writer inherits, refines, or extends, but also the factors conditioning the author's personal behavior and the nature of that behavior itself. For example, Dryden's various prefaces betray not only his involvement with certain controversies and the powers of mind he brings to them, but also his anger, pettiness, and self-defensiveness. That is, the response is a kind of illocutionary act and thus at once a circumstance of its occasion and a kind of behavior. In coming to know the occasion and its circumstances through the writing, we also learn about extrapoetic personality. The extent to which our knowledge of the personal behavior of authors, our knowledge of biography in the *Lives*, hinges upon circumstantial inquiry has yet to be explored systematically, but it seems evident, to me at least, that the bulk of what we know about the extrapoetic personalities of, say, Milton, Dryden, Pope, and Addison is directly attributable to Johnson's exposition of and inferences from the circumstances of one form of writing or another. Of course, the circumstantial approach is most immediately useful to an assessment of powers in relation to past accomplishments.

Finally, as a critic, Johnson is concerned with the moral, social, and political tendencies of works; with the larger ramifications of works as representations or expressions of truth and reality and, thus, as influences on readers' conceptions of life; in short, with all those aspects of works, considered apart from their technical and formal excellence, that oblige us to consider the author in terms of the moral feelings or the view of things that he promotes, encourages, or implies. Here Johnson is chiefly interested in the author's representation of life, in the truth or probability of his statements and representations, in the complexity or simplicity of his view of nature and human relations, and in the potential of his works to mislead understanding or misdirect conduct. Central to Johnson's judgments of all the poets—Does this poet speak like a man of this world? Can this emphasis on love be credited? Is this probable under the circumstances?—this aspect of Johnson's criticism in the *Lives* has not been thoroughly examined. Yet our apprehension of the poets as distinctive individuals depends to a great extent on Johnson's concern with the social, moral, and political proclivities of their works.

In my working text of the *Lives*, I have more or less diligently noted in the margins the points where Johnson's statements can be seen as implicit answers to the questions entailed by the categories of critical emphasis outlined above. My not very surprising discovery is that a single sentence or paragraph often participates in all three and that the marks are rather evenly distributed throughout the biographies, mute confirmation perhaps of Lipking's notion that the *Lives* is "literary criticism based on the criticism of life," a kind of "conduct book."[34] It is perhaps only slightly impertinent to suggest that no study of Johnson's conception of the relation between the life and the writings of the poet can proceed effectively in the absence of a clear understanding of the peculiar qualitative emphases of his approach to art (and, of course, any other product of human endeavor). At any rate, with such an understanding we can clearly see that the *Lives* is less an outpouring of "aperçus," a "restless movement from point to point," than a series of statements of great variety regulated by a coherent set of concerns, and that for Johnson writing is variously significant as action and as a sign or expression of mind and behavior. Furthermore, such an understanding is prerequisite to the following discussion of life and writing, in which reflection on Johnson's practice is filtered through the categories of authorship discriminated by Wayne Booth in *Critical Understanding*.[35] Booth provides us with useful terms for our intuitive perceptions, our intuitive distinctions. In what follows, then, Booth's differentiations will have as their controlling context Johnson's practice and the immediately preceding description of his intellectual framework. Finally, of Booth's five authors— real, dramatized, implied, career, and public—I shall concentrate only on the first four.

At the center of the diversified complex is the real-life *writer*, the "*flesh-and-blood person*, a man or woman who writes only sometimes and who otherwise lives a more or less troubled or happy life."[36] In a real sense, this person—a complex of conflicting sensations, ideas, impulses, of metabolic, neural, autonomic processes, of decisions and indecisions, of physical growth and decay, of pains, aches, pleasures—is finally unknowable to others and to the self, except superficially in analytic *disjecta membra*. It is perhaps interesting to note that this person, the ground of all writing and all personally significant action, has no character; this person rather moves than acts, and in the course of any day spends most of his time running on automatic, performing the routine tasks necessary to successful negotiation with the largely predictable challenges of quotidian existence. Here is variety, contradiction, and insignificance in full foliation. By paying careful attention to the real-life writer day after day, we may discern in or impose upon his diversity certain regularities or consistencies and come to know something about the characteristic, distinctive, or peculiar. But if Johnson thought "that there has rarely passed a life of which a judicious and faithful narrative would not be useful" (*Rambler* 60), he also knew that "the greater part of mankind 'have no character at all,' have little that distinguishes them from others equally good or bad" (*Lives* 3:263-64). Character is a function of choice and habit (i.e., behavior, once chosen or allowed, which now chooses us), and it is by activity that we distinguish ourselves, especially when it actualizes our desires, goals, values, when it signalizes the desirability of this or that. And since geniuses (and all others) can turn with equal ease to the east or to the west, and since they bring their whole minds with them in whichever direction they turn, they can be expected to reveal themselves in all that they do deliberately or habitually, and perhaps nowhere more importantly than in their primary roles. If the characters of soldiers are formed or revealed on the battlefield and those of bankers in their management of funds, then those of authors are exhibited in their writings.

It has been suggested that writing, while "in some ways an action like any other, is a privileged act, one in which a man can temporarily insulate himself against the thousand natural shocks that flesh is heir to."[37] Useful as such a reminder is, it is also necessary to remember that most of our significant acts are similarly privileged, in the sense that, however closely tied to emergent "reality," they allow for deliberation and choice. Moreover, the privilege, where it exists and is singular to writing, is often an added dividend, inasmuch as it makes possible significant choice unencumbered by any accidental circumstances that might obscure or distort characteristic behavior. The man of large learning and great comprehension of mind who comes into company without the social graces and argumentative skills necessary to the easy give and take of conversational interchange may disgrace the abilities that distinguish him, and yet, though social ineptitude may form some part of his character, it would be foolish to subsume his general character under his particular social performance. Special circumstances and pressing exigencies may rather deflect than reflect the distinctive bent of genius. What perhaps needs to be emphasized is not that writing is a privileged act, but that in any piece of writing (or in any significant act) a writer can reveal only so much of his character (or of his personality, his view of things, his age, or whatever) as the task immediately before him makes possible. In no single work can he express all that he may want to say or all that he has the capacity to say because of the kind of character he is, but only what the exigencies of the work before him allow. Thus, the writer whom we cannot in any ultimate sense know leads us to knowable authors.

In the first circle beyond the writer we can isolate for inspection the "dramatized author," the "I" who vocalizes all lyrics, speaks in many narratives, and expresses himself in letters. It is here most probably that we meet the "Thomson" that the lady of Savage's acquaintance confuses with James Thomson. Only the very naive and unsophisticated reader assumes a necessary correspondence between this "I" and the writer. Nevertheless, there is also no necessary disjunction between the two. Prior to reading we can make no absolute claims about similarity or disparity, for the dramatized "I" may subsist in relation to the writer as twin, brother, friend, neighbor, or alien. Between the "I" of the *Elegy Written in a Country Churchyard* or *Tintern Abbey* and Gray or Wordsworth, for example, a line of distinction would, in most respects, be superfluous, for the poems may be considered as outward and visible manifestations of the personal feelings or views of the writer, whereas between the "I" dramatized in Pope's letters and Alexander Pope we have a space cleared by ingenuousness but occupied by "affectation and ambition" (*Lives* 3:208), the "I" here wearing a semitransparent mask. Clearly, Johnson regularly expects the "I" at least to shadow forth the writer, especially when the "I" speaks on occasions—in love verses and elegies, for example—that are presumably important to the writer in his personal and private capacity. In such cases, Johnson is quick to call attention to a failure in the *writer* to create an "I" adequate to the motivating circumstance, the judgment of lack of sincerity serving, thus, as a secondary but inevitable reflection on perceived artistic flaws. Although the text often reveals a gap between writer and "I," the text is not always perfidious. To avoid confusing writer and "I" Johnson must often go to extrinsic evidence to determine identity or its absence. In reacting to the gap between Pope and the "I" of Pope's letters, for example, Johnson depends not only on internal inconsistencies or "unconscious" implications, but on that richly complex but relatively stable conception of Pope to which anecdotes and his other writings have contributed. Johnson is no naive reader, but he is open, flexible, and wise enough to recognize that the dramatized "I" often speaks the interests, opinions, and real preferences of the writer, sometimes directly, sometimes implicitly.

Beyond the dramatized is the *implied* author. The author who is always and inescapably present in writing is the implied author, the "creating person who is implied by the totality of a given work when it is offered to the world."[38] Whatever values, emphases, degrees or kinds of learning, sophistication, genius, judgment, imagination, whatever tones, points of view, attitudes toward life inhere in the text as implications of artistic choices depend upon and reflect the implied author. Repeatedly in the *Lives*, Johnson focuses on texts as signs of the implied author, taking up learning, genius, imagination, judgment, level of diction, nature, and so on, not to satisfy the ends of grammatical, technical, or formal criticism, but to disclose the manifest, operational components of intellectual and moral capacity. The qualitative, circumstantial, and moral aspects of Johnson's criticism are exhibited in full power in his analysis of the implied author. Of the *Tale of a Tub*, for example, Johnson says that "it exhibits a vehemence and rapidity of mind, a copiousness of images, and vivacity of diction . . . " (*Lives* 3:51). This statement, two-thirds of which refers ostensibly to the work but of which the whole has reference directly or tacitly to Swift, is but a local stop on the route of Johnson's criticism. To Johnson, the acts and choices embedded in the text are direct indicators of authorial powers. At the level of manifest power, the correspondence between author and work is absolute. The capacity of the author is directly displayed; genius, learning, powers of mind cannot be simulated or faked.

On the other hand, it is apparent that morality can be "faked," that the gap between the morality of the implied author and that of the writer can be great or small (small to the

point of virtual nonexistence). Johnson has no reason to suspect, for example, that Addison deformed in his personal life
the morality expressed or implied in his works. Certainly some
writers profess better than they live; just as "heroic implied
authors can be created by cowards,"[39] so openhearted implied
authors can come from the pens of egoistic bullies. Johnson's
recognition of this potential disparity between the values of
the implied author and those of the "real" writer is stated often
and variously. In *Rambler* 14, for example, he notes that there is
"often [not always, but often] a striking contrariety between
the life of an author and his writings"; and in the *Life of Savage*
he remarks that Savage was rather the friend of virtue than a
good man. To determine degree of correspondence here
Johnson often has to rely on additional information, supplied
either by other works or by external evidence. Nevertheless,
independently of supplementary testimonies, Johnson can frequently determine much from the text itself. First, the implied
author (who has, of course, the same name as the writer) is
responsible for the whole of any given work, for what it says
both openly and covertly; thus, the values, ethical qualities,
and moral tendencies of the work are unequivocally his. The
writer, through the agency of the implied author, directly
discloses his knowledge of the "right" and the complexity,
simplicity, sophistication, and so forth of his moral comprehension. If from other sources a gap between profession
and practice is known to exist, then for Johnson the issue is one
of determining kind of culpability within a range extending
from hypocrisy to pardonable, though perhaps not excusable,
frailty. And Johnson is regularly willing to soften the charge of
hypocrisy by acknowledging that at the time of writing the
poet believed what he wrote, believed himself capable of performing in conformity with the virtues he ascribed to himself.[40] Hence, though morality may be faked, knowledge of its
nature and imperatives cannot. And even from the "faking" of
morality we can learn something important about the author's
moral sensibility.

Second, it may not be true that, as Aristotle suggested, the
decision to write comedy or tragedy is a necessary con-

sequence of the poet's character, but surely the decision to write this or that kind of work can reveal something about the author's conception of himself, about his willingness to be measured by certain standards, and about his readiness to struggle against one pattern of excellence or another. The very act of writing on this occasion, in this genre, in this tone, to this person—friend or antagonist—may reveal characteristic moral behavior. For example, the very act of engaging in dispute with Settle, apart from the substance of his attacks, tells us something about Dryden's proud self-defensiveness. And, curiously, Milton's various prose pieces are significant to Johnson less for what they tell us about Milton's politics or religion than for what they disclose of his particular kind of surly independence.

Finally, the moral self has a way of peeping through its disguise. The poet may protest too much; he may be inconsistent, or the fit may be too snug to restrain the characteristic yelp. For example, try as he will, Pope cannot avoid betraying in his letters the self he is eager to conceal; he represents rather what he "wished his state of mind to appear" than what it characteristically was. In spite of his efforts to be easy and natural, Pope writes letters that are "premeditated and artificial" and that show an inability to free himself from the "affectation and ambition" that even he thought perverted the "epistolary integrity" (*Lives* 3:208) of his early letters.[41] In the letters, the dramatized author and the implied author often coexist in a state of uneasy tension. (As an aside, it is worth noting that "good" writing can, in some respects, make the good man. Life imitates art to the extent that the act of projecting a moral self imposes obligations on the man to live in conformity with what is implicated in professed values; thus, writing is often self-defining, a form of self-subsumption whereby projected images of the self coerce or encourage behavior adapted to them.) Regardless of the frequent disparities between the professions and the practices of the writer, the writings are often Johnson's (and our) most valuable resource for determining not only intellectual but moral sensibility and behavior.

In the last circle (at least the last that I shall discuss) is the "career author," "the sustained creative [agent] implied by a *sequence* of implied authors,"[42] who, like the other authors, lives in more or less loving contiguity with the "flesh-and-blood writer." This is the author found in the various "characters" of the *Lives*, the comprehensive entity that serves as the conceptual basis of Johnson's large, general assessments, the predominant image, established by the evidence in the aggregate. Although chronologically last in this discussion, the career author was probably the logically first condition of Johnson's undertaking; he brought his views about most of the poets with him; he did not find them as he wrote. In all likelihood, he adjusted information newly acquired, or newly reinforced by rereading, to a previously established, functional, complex but relatively stable conception of the poet's capacities and powers (and of the standards of excellence that a succession of endeavors had established in the various kinds of composition). What is true of general experience is similarly true of literary experience: "As we see more, we become possessed of more certainties, and consequently gain more principles of reasoning, and found a wider basis of analogy."[43] Johnson undoubtedly came to his task, not only with his categories of interest, but with his inductively formed, controlling conceptions of individual and collective achievement firmly in place. At any rate, it seems clear that Johnson's synthesizing constructs function throughout the *Lives* as the bases of evaluation and as the certifiers of probability.

It has been argued that when Johnson educes personal qualities, whether social or moral, from the traits of works, he almost always has "empirical evidence" from independent sources "to support his interpretation."[44] That is, Johnson is very cautious about reading life from literature and generally seeks to buttress inference with independently established fact. Johnson certainly looks before leaping, but repeatedly in the *Lives* Johnson moves with equal ease from text to life and from life to text. Throughout his accounts of the poets we find instances of *reciprocal implication*, with the artistic trait sometimes finding its corollary in the personal history, and with the "historical" trait sometimes finding a parallel exemplification in the writing. In *Milton*, Johnson moves from a perceived "Turkish contempt of females" in the works to a discussion of Milton's treatment of his daughters, whereas in *Swift* he "confirms" the reports of the roughness of Swift's manner with servants by the testimony of the writings, taken at large. "To his domesticks he was naturally rough; and a man of a rigorous temper, with that vigilance of minute attention which his works discover, *must have been* a master that few could bear" (*Lives* 3:56, my emphasis). It is interesting that although Johnson has conflicting evidence for Swift's behavior toward his servants from surviving anecdotes, he gives credence to the negative, presumably because it squares not only with what Swift says elsewhere in nonpoetic contexts, but with what is inferable from the nature of his works (and possibly because it forms a logical nexus with other undisputed aspects of his personality, his "oriental scrupulosity," for example).

It would be difficult—perhaps impossible—to determine with certainty whether Johnson found his warrant for the "personal" inference from the writing in empirical evidence, whether reciprocal implication was a necessary or usual prior condition of judgment, or whether a perceived "personal" quality in the writing provided the warrant for the inclusion of an anecdote. What is noteworthy, however, is that we very rarely find a morally significant anecdote, a distinguishing piece of "empirical evidence," that is not consonant with the moral or intellectual sensibility revealed by the writing. Almost never. And given the antecedent security of Johnson's conception of poetic and intellectual character, based on his familiarity with the writings, it is reasonable to suppose that the credibility of empirical evidence was tested against established human probabilities and, more important, Johnson's working understanding of the career author. Partial support for this position is provided by the number of instances in which Johnson—using the circumstantial method in reverse, as it were—"creates" events by treating mature achievement as the circumstantial basis of antecedent or possible behavior: considering the nature of Savage's works, "it is *very reasonable to conjecture* that his *application* [to his juvenile studies, about which Johnson knows nothing directly] was equal to his *abilities*" (*Lives* 2:325, my emphases). Moreover, Johnson expects the same quality and power of mind to be displayed, albeit in proportionate degrees, throughout the scenes of life. Following the passage just cited, Johnson says, "*Nor can it be doubted*, that if his earliest productions had been preserved . . . *we might have found* vigorous sallies of that sprightly humour which distinguishes *The Author to be let*, and in others strong touches of that ardent imagination which painted the solemn scenes of *The Wanderer*" (my emphases).

The prevalence of a controlling conception of the essential nature of the poet is everywhere apparent, but perhaps most strikingly in those instances where Johnson confronts the anomalous or doubtful. To Johnson, for example, Swift's *Tale of a Tub* deviates markedly from his other works, displaying qualities not consonant with those of his career achievement. "His *Tale of a Tub* has little resemblance to his other pieces. It exhibits a vehemence and rapidity of mind . . . such as he afterwards never possessed or never exerted" (*Lives* 3:51). With regard to the question of whether or not Addison was the author of *The Drummer*, Johnson decides the issue by trusting the report of Steele and, more important, by measuring the performance against the yardstick of the career author. "To the opinion of Steele may be added the proof supplied by the play itself, of which the characters are such as Addison *would have delineated* and the tendency *such as* Addison *would have promoted*" (*Lives* 2:106, my emphases). And what Johnson does here with *The Drummer* and *Tale of a Tub* he does also, in my view, with the empirical evidence; i.e., he establishes its probable validity on a scale, in one dish of which is an assayed weight of value determined by Johnson's controlling image of the man, as derived primarily from the writings.

Still, Johnson generally refuses to "cook" the data, to adjust unimpeachable facts to the exigencies of his hypothesis. His is not a petty mind determined to make, against the evidence, a foolish consistency. Whenever clear disproportion between one and another form of action rears its evidentiary head,

Johnson honestly registers it. In Boswell's *Life*, Johnson is recorded as saying, in reference to James Beattie's conversation, that "it is wonderful . . . what a difference there sometimes is between a man's powers of writing and talking." Similarly, in the *Life of Congreve*, Johnson remarks, "It cannot be observed without wonder that a mind so vigorous and fertile in dramatick compositions should on any other occasion discover nothing but impotence and poverty" (*Lives* 2:229). The facts are inescapable, but note that to Johnson they are *wonderful;* they are both true *and* strange, undeniable *and* unusual. Johnson clearly expects the consonance he does not find. Throughout the *Lives*, Johnson uses cautiously and judiciously (but nevertheless persistently) his earned sense of the career author to evaluate particular biographical and textual details. He attends to the details *from* the perspective of the career author.

Like so much of this essay, the foregoing account of "authors" and of what they may tell us about how Johnson perceives relationships between life and writing is, of course, propaedeutic and suggestive. Any full study of the *Lives* would need to refine and complicate each of the "author" categories, exploring the subdivisions that Johnson's text forced upon analysis. But as we focus on the principles and assumptions that underlie and govern Johnson's thinking about art and life and on their relevance to his "characteristic linkage of biography and criticism," we gain, I think, a richer understanding of the artistic integrity of particular lives and of the *Lives* in general. Great would be my satisfaction and surprise if what I now say of the foregoing discussion could be granted a portion of the credit and authority that we readily give to Johnson's remarks—here adapted to my purpose—following his speculative commentary on Dryden's learning: "Of all this, however, if the proof be demanded, I cannot now undertake to give it; the atoms of probability lie scattered over all the lives; by him who thinks the question worth his notice, the lives must be perused with very close attention" (see *Lives* 1:418).

Nevertheless, when all the work is done, we will still be

faced with a monumental piece of literature that in whole and in part is not structured according to any single principle or set of principles to which we could accommodate any other biography. Moreover, the accounts of the poets are variously structured, some lacking one or more of the three major parts,[45] some containing more than the three (long digressions on matters of importance to the history of ideas, to the progress of a work, and so on; distinct intellectual and poetic characters; etc.), and some barely making up lives at all. From the collection as a whole, however, we can make out the outline of the principal, prototypical, but perhaps never perfectly realized, structural plan. After a brief account of birth, education, and any other "facts" of early life, Johnson proceeds with a chronological survey of the writings, interspersing the narrative with critical commentary and the citation of relevant "historical" or "personal" events coeval with the writings; then describes in a separate section the intellectual character of the poet, which both epitomizes what is diffusely exhibited in the biographical section and prepares the way for what follows; and, finally, examines the artistic production, focusing on primary works as distinct realizations of specific powers and capacities and as specialized reflections of intellectual character, and concluding the whole with a poetic character. Thus, the intellectual character is the crucial link between biography and criticism, the unit of mediation necessary to prefaces that are both biographical and critical. There is, in short, an underlying structural logic to the lives, notwithstanding its diverse exemplification or its frequent appearance in vestigial or embryonic forms.

But, again, the *Lives* is finally sui generis. If biography as we have come to know it is a species of narrative, governed by some principle of "progressive" form, obedient to the demands of a developing theme or story, then it neither derives its structural impetus from nor finds its structural origin in Johnson's lives, which are paratactic, not progressive, in structure. Biography went in directions that do not radiate from Johnson as center. Yet it is still fair to say that Johnson is central to biography. With Richard Altick, we can agree that "he showed his age [and subsequent generations] what a biography should contain."[46] And if he did not build as his successors did, his "failure" cannot be ascribed to a lack of those "integrating, shaping talents that the very greatest artists in biography should possess,"[47] or to a dearth of facts, the bricks of biography. No, "by an easy metaphor," what "was said of Rome, adorned by Augustus," and of poetry, "embellished by Dryden," may be applied to biography beautified by Johnson: "he found it brick, and he left it marble." Johnson built in his own way, and the reasons why he built differently and why he neither is nor can be imitated are not far to seek. He satisfied (indeed, transcended) the demands implicit in the immediate task set for him by the booksellers and produced prefaces for a rival edition of the poets, *and* he brought to the undertaking his whole mind, creating in the end a work that has many coherent parts (lives) but that depends for its enduring power and value on the genius and comprehension of its author, to whom we make silent reference as we read.

As we read the *Lives*, we are engaged, as we are in no other biography to a comparable degree, as much with the biographer as with his subjects. As we read, we learn a great deal about men and the products and affairs of men, but, more important, we make continual reference from the work to the man responsible for it. We read the *Lives* in the way that Johnson reads the poetry of his poets, with a sense of the man behind the work. We are, in an untrivial sense, "Johnsonized" by the text. Johnson's kind of criticism has its way with us, as we inadvertently fulfill its imperatives in our experience of the text. We are engaged in a form of what Michael Polanyi has called "tacit understanding," which always involves our depending on one kind of awareness to attend to something else (e.g., we attend *to* the events at the end of the stick we hold in our hand *from* a tacit awareness of events in the palm of our hand).[48] In our reading of the *Lives*, we attend *to* what Johnson has to say about men and writings *from* an understanding of Johnson's genius; i.e., we read about, say, Pope *from* a developing conception of Johnson, and in the process, we learn something that we feel is genuinely "true" about both Pope and

Johnson. Just as Johnson attends *to* the details of Pope's life and writings *from* a tacit conception of the essential Pope, so we attend *to* the details of the lives *from* a developing conception of the implied Johnson. Johnson is always various, but rarely surprising (i.e., an olio of incompatible traits and judgments). If, upon reflection, we attend to Johnson, then we bring forward into notice the particular details of commentary upon which our tacit understanding was based. We read the man from his writing, and what enchains us is not any local or grand architectonic accomplishment, but an implied author, whom we have come to recognize and admire (in spite of our resistance to some of his judgments). Johnson, who has taught us to see in writing a kind of conduct, writes a work that, like the *Rambler* essays, comes to seem (as one critic has said of Goldsmith's *Citizen of the World*) "a kind of conduct, a way of [confronting] the world that sets us a model of what it might mean" and of what it would require "to cope" intelligently and reasonably "with the world's various opportunities, problems, woes."[49] Thus, even as Johnson activates our energies, setting before us a model of performance in an engaging display of assertive humanism, he also forces the recognition that in the long march of biography, "nobody can be said to put you in mind of Johnson." "Let us go to the next best:—there is nobody."[50]

JOHN A. DUSSINGER

Dr. Johnson's Solemn Response to Beneficence

One of the most eloquent testimonies of human behavior anywhere in Johnson's writing appears in his *Account of the Life of Mr. Richard Savage* (1744), after the narrative of the murder trial, when Savage finds begging in the street the very woman who had perjured herself against him and divides his last guinea with her: "This is an Action which in some Ages would have made a Saint, and perhaps in others a Hero, and which, without any hyperbolical Encomiums, must be allowed to be an Instance of uncommon Generosity, an Act of complicated Virtue; by which he at once relieved the Poor, corrected the Vicious, and forgave an Enemy; by which he at once remitted the strongest Provocations, and exercised the most ardent Charity."[1] Although denouncing the woman's motives, Johnson does not question the innocence of the benefactor and extols the action beyond anything else his erstwhile friend accomplished in his pathetic career. In spite of our effort to reconstitute the historical text, the emotion connected here with the giving of money is probably inaccessible to the modern reader, for whom both the word *charity* and the action itself (in our society usually tax deductible) are denied any religious significance. Yet the lofty merit attributed to Savage implies a world where indifference to human misery is the norm. This selfishness was rooted in the classical economic system, which, Lucien Goldmann has observed, had effectually "deconsecrated" the medieval ethic concerning both usury and charity: "Poverty was perhaps not universally regarded as a sin, but it was no longer thought a condition pleasing to God."[2] Hence, we are to understand that Savage, by sharing his last coin with the woman, surpassed all expectations of even a Christian performing his duty toward the poor.[3]

As if invoking St. Francis's example of reinstating medieval contemptus mundi in a world of Renaissance bankers, Johnson was unusual among his contemporaries in embracing a deeply religious ideal of charity. Emma Woodhouse's frosty advice was a much easier attitude to accept: "If we feel for the wretched, enough to do all we can for them, the rest is empty sympathy, only distressing to ourselves."[4] By contrast we have the spectacle of Johnson continually distressing himself over the plight of the poor, even to the extent of carrying home on his back a sick prostitute he finds lying helpless in the street: "He had her taken care of with all tenderness for a long time, at considerable expence, till she was restored to health, and endeavoured to put her into a virtuous way of living."[5] In an age when public charities were being founded by appeals to the selfish interests of the donor, Johnson both astonished and embarrassed such close observers as Boswell and Mrs. Thrale. Mrs. Desmoulins, we are told, "found an asylum in the house of her old friend, whose doors were always open to the unfortunate, and who well observed the precept of the Gospel, for he 'was kind to the unthankful and to the evil.' "[6] Savage's action, wholly unselfish, performed without any expectation of gratitude or indebtedness in one who had been his enemy, is a rare instance of what Johnson strove for in his own spiritual life, as indicated in his diaries, "in the general exercise and cultivation of benevolence."[7]

A variety of narrative stances, ranging from Olympian detachment to fraternal sympathy, complicates this story of the distressed poet; but from beginning to end, Savage's moral plight is measured in financial terms: "He had now no longer any Hopes of Assistance from his Friends at *Bristol*, who as

Merchants, and by Consequence sufficiently studious of Profit, cannot be supposed to have look'd with much Compassion upon Negligence and Extravagance, or to think any Excellence equivalent to a Fault of such Consequence as Neglect of Oeconomy" (120–21). Given a radically egocentric environment, the individual's best hope is to fend for himself and so avoid as far as possible the indebtedness that inevitably leads to prison. But in Savage's case a prudential self-interest, no matter how desirable, was temperamentally beyond reach; and without quite denigrating the commercial system that eventually incarcerated his friend and brought on an untimely death, Johnson nevertheless implies the need of charity lest we "become as sounding brass, or a tinkling cymbal" like those "sufficiently studious of Profit."

Selfishness had political as well as economic significance in the age of Walpole. "Severity towards the poor was, in Johnson's opinion . . . , an undoubted and constant attendant or consequence upon whiggism."[8] In the *Life of Addison* Johnson attacks the *Spectator* for its contemptuous attitude as expressed through Sir Andrew Freeport, but notes Freeport's subsequent amelioration: "Steele had made [Freeport], in the true spirit of unfeeling commerce, declare that he 'would not build an hospital for idle people'; but at last he buys land, settles in the country, and builds not a manufactory, but an hospital for twelve old husbandmen, for men with whom a merchant has little acquaintance, and whom he commonly considers with little kindness."[9] While safely removed from the sentimental tone of later writers on social ills (Goldsmith, Sterne, Brooke, and Mackenzie, for instance), Johnson's biography of Savage stresses the portentous affect of giving aid unconditionally in a world where the profit motive and laissez-faire policies of the Whig government threaten to increase the misery of the poor.

At issue in the *Life of Savage*, then, is how to reconcile, if possible, the glorification of the hero's charity, on the one hand, with the moral attack on both his "voluntary delusion" and his contemporaries' selfish behavior, on the other. In what remains the most systematic analysis of Johnson's ethical writing, Paul Alkon provides a gloss for our specific inquiry here: "Johnson's immense reach of sympathetic understanding has not yet been sufficiently appreciated."[10] Yet even an assiduous ferreting out of opinions expressed in the *Rambler, Adventurer, Idler,* and other texts fails to reveal the alignment of that "sympathetic understanding" with the author's rationalistic morality. Alkon finds Johnson, like Machiavelli, Hobbes, Mandeville, and modern anthropologists, deeply committed to defining social behavior according to principles of self-interest; but he also finds him quite opposed to this "selfish" tradition when ascribing benevolence to Christian piety and hence pitting medieval charity against modern usury.[11]

Once we see the supreme importance of the "divinely irrational impulse" in Johnson's moral thought, his concern with self-assessment as a guide to living in the world is really secondary. What is remarkable in *Savage,* in fact, is the narrator's emphasis on the need of an opiate to ease the horror of poverty: "[Savage] proceeded throughout his Life to tread the same Steps on the same Circle; always applauding his past Conduct, or at least forgetting it, to amuse himself with Phantoms of Happiness, which were dancing before him; and willingly turned his Eyes from the Light of Reason, when it would have discovered the Illusion, and shewn him, what he never wished to see, his real State" (74). So effective was Savage's resilience under misfortune that at least for this purpose he could evince "a philosophical Mind, and very properly [be] proposed to the Imitation of Multitudes, who, for want of diverting their Imaginations with the same Dexterity, languish under Afflictions which might be easily removed" (73). Paradoxically, illusions are sometimes necessary to relieve the pain of one's "real State." So are "sweeteners." Upon hearing the complaint that money given to the poor is only wasted on gin or tobacco, Johnson retorted, "Life is a pill which none of us can bear to swallow without gilding; yet for the poor we delight in stripping it still barer, and are not ashamed to shew even visible displeasure, if ever the bitter taste is taken from their mouths."[12] According to this same illusional principle, he traces Addison's addiction to alcohol to weaknesses in personality: "In the bottle, discontent seeks for comfort, cowardice for courage, and bashfulness for confidence. It is not unlikely that Addison was first seduced to excess by the manumission which he obtained from the servile timidity of his sober hours."[13]

Despite his obvious failings, Savage "must be considered upon the whole as a Benefactor to the World; nor can his personal Example do any hurt, since whoever hears of his Faults, will hear of the Miseries which they brought upon him, and which would deserve less Pity, had not his Condition been such as made his Faults pardonable" (75). Johnson never doubts the moral value of Savage's writings, which, "being the Productions of Study, uniformly tended to the Exaltation of the Mind" (75); and without attempting to exonerate his friend of his more reprehensible conduct, he nevertheless stresses the early deprivations that obviate any judgments according to the usual adult standards: "He may be considered as a Child *exposed* to all the Temptations of Indigence, at an Age when Resolution was not yet strengthened by Conviction, nor Virtue confirmed by Habit" (75). Beyond all his notoriously self-ingratiating behavior, one attribute continually redeems him in this biography: "Compassion was indeed the distinguishing Quality of *Savage*" (41). As if to suggest an environmental influence on his charitableness, the narrative emphasizes the many acts of kindness (performed first by such women as Lady Mason, Mrs. Lloyd, Mrs. Oldfield, and the Countess of Hertford; later by such literary friends as Steele, Wilkes, Hill, and Pope; and finally by Mr. Dagg, the sympathetic keeper at the Bristol prison) that gave him relief from the predators who endangered his life from the outset. Clearly, in a world regulated by the monetary principle of credit/debit (the equivalent of the Law in the Old Testament), the impoverished individual needs more than the Light of Reason to aid him through his tribulations: without charity in the medieval sense poverty is tantamount to enslavement under whiggish political and economic conditions.

An attack on the hero's enemies is one way of mitigating his culpability as a moral agent in the story. As Boswell remarked, Johnson was so partial to Savage that he did not hesitate to believe Savage's account of his mother's treatment of him, and vehemently castigated Lady Macclesfield, still living at the time of composition, for her unnatural cruelty to her son.[14] Leaving aside the matter of the unknowable truth, we are primarily concerned with how the biographer viewed his subject; and one discrepancy in the facts illustrates how closely Johnson wrote himself into the life. Boswell refers to "a letter from Savage, after Lord Tyrconnel had discarded him, addressed to the Reverend Mr. Gilbert, his Lordship's Chaplain, in which he requests him in the humblest manner, to represent his case to the Viscount."[15] But according to Johnson, Savage's supposed "noble pride" prevented him from seeking a reconciliation. No friend himself to patrons, Johnson supplies by indirect discourse his hero's blunt reply to Lord Tyrconnel "that his Resentment was only a Plea for the Violation of his Promise: He asserted that he had done nothing that ought to exclude him from that Subsistence which he thought not so much a Favour, as a Debt, since it was offered him upon Conditions, which he had never broken; and that his only Fault was, that he could not be supported with nothing" (61).

Johnson's faith in Savage's aristocratic origins was essential to his sympathetic view of Savage's rebellious behavior. In fact, had he ever suspected his friend of having been an imposter (as Boswell did), he probably could not have written this biography at all. In spite of his own humble background he held a deep respect for social rank and deplored the opportunism associated with whiggish upstarts. Against Dr. Taylor's plea on behalf of Mungo Campbell, who shot the Earl of Eglintoune, " 'A poor man has as much honour as a rich man; and Campbell had *that* to defend' "; Johnson's reply was " 'A poor man has no honour.' "[16]

Yet a meritocracy, rather than a hereditary privileged class, is the ideal underlying the "noble pride" of Johnson and Savage alike. We remember how at Oxford Johnson "was too proud to accept money, and somebody having set a pair of new shoes at his door, he threw them away with indignation."[17] It is this

same ferocious independence in poverty that he attributes to
Savage, a spirit justifiable in view of his friend's poetic genius
as well as supposed birth.

> He acknowledged, that Lord *Tyrconnel* often exhorted
> him to regulate his Method of Life, and not to spend all his
> Nights in Taverns, and that he appeared very desirous,
> that he would pass those Hours with him which he so
> freely bestowed upon others. This Demand Mr. *Savage*
> considered as a Censure of his Conduct, which he could
> never patiently bear; and which even in the latter and
> cooler Part of his Life was so offensive to him, that he
> declared it as his Resolution, *to spurn that Friend who
> should presume to dictate to him*; and it is not likely, that in
> his earlier Years he received Admonitions with more
> Calmness. [61]

While acknowledging his friend's precipitous ingratitude,
Johnson nevertheless does not blame him for his resentment of
Tyrconnel's possessiveness ("the Request was still more unrea-
sonable, as the Company to which he was to have been con-
fined was insupportably disagreeable"). When both were
penniless but proud, Johnson walked with Savage around St.
James's Square one night for lack of a bed to sleep in: "they
were not at all depressed by their situation; but in high spirits
and brimful of patriotism, traversed the square for several
hours, inveighed against the minister, and 'resolved they
would *stand by their country.*' "[18] From the biographer's point
of view, Savage's effrontery toward Tyrconnel reveals the evil
of patronage itself. (Besides his well-known answer to Lord
Chesterfield, Johnson could not resist inserting an opinionated
definition of *patron* in the *Dictionary*: "Commonly a wretch
who supports with insolence, and is paid with flattery.")[19] In
refusing to play the servile role expected of him, even to the
extent of sacrificing all further support, Savage may have been
foolish under the circumstances; but Johnson cannot help but
identify himself with Savage in his sense of outrage at a benefactor's presumption to lay claim to gratitude. This attitude

irked Mrs. Piozzi: "No man, therefore, who smarted from the ingratitude of his friends, found any sympathy from our philosopher: 'Let him do good on higher motives next time,' would be the answer; 'he will then be sure of his reward.' "[20]

Since, as Johnson freely acknowledged, he never courted patronage and thus was not really familiar with the upper classes, Savage was valuable to him as a source of information.[21] The narrator hints darkly that while in Lord Tyrconnel's graces, Savage used the opportunity to gain insight into the ways of the aristocracy and to find "whether great Men were selected for high Stations, or high Stations made great Men." Like a secret agent, the hero penetrated the circles of the most powerful and through close observation and discernment became "a Critic on human Life" (64). Instead of reporting any details of Savage's privileged knowledge, however, Johnson pleads uncharacteristically that "it may not be entirely safe to relate, because the Persons whose Characters he criticised are powerful; and Power and Resentment are seldom Strangers" (65). But in a possible allusion to Walpole, Savage is briefly cast as an Imlac or a Lien Chi Altangi.

> It may however be observed, that he did not appear to have formed very elevated Ideas of those to whom the Administration of Affairs, or the Conduct of Parties, has been intrusted; who have been considered as the Advocates of the Crown, or the Guardians of the People, and who have obtained the most implicit Confidence, and the loudest Applauses. Of one particular Person, who has been at one Time so popular as to be generally esteemed, and at another so formidable as to be universally detested, he observed, that his Acquisitions had been small, or that his Capacity was narrow, and that the whole Range of his Mind was from Obscenity to Politics, and from Politics to Obscenity. [65]

In the context of the morally corrupt patronage system, the hero's self-assertiveness deals a well-deserved blow to aristocratic arrogance. "*Savage* however was not one of those, who suffer themselves to be injured without Resistance" (69). The quarrel with Tyrconnel becomes a contest between the literary power of "Wit and Virulence" and the politico-economic power of privileged class, as Tyrconnel is reduced to hiring ruffians ("that did no Honour to his Courage") for the purpose of giving the hero a beating at a coffeehouse. Despite the hardships that ensue from this cause célèbre, Savage appears to emerge as a champion, whose "Superiority of Wit supplied the Disadvantages of his Fortune" (70).

Savage later incorporated this triumph into his *Poem on Public Spirit* (which Johnson describes favorably), in which he testifies to "the natural Equality of Mankind, and endeavour[s] to suppress that Pride which inclines Men to imagine that Right is the Consequence of Power" (93). Notwithstanding his sincere Christian piety, Johnson, as Alkon observed, also embraces "the most fundamental form of self-interest: the desire for personal happiness."[22] In this respect, he is much closer to Jefferson or Franklin, say, than to St. Teresa of Avila or St. John of the Cross, whose self-abnegation ("In order to arrive at possessing everything / Desire to possess nothing"[23]) went completely against the grain of classical economics. C.S. Lewis has charged that Johnson advocated the individualism that diminished Christianity to "theological hedonism," with the mercenary doctrine of future rewards and punishments its ultimate expression.[24] If so, Johnson was in this regard well in step with the discourse of his age. In general, the idea of self-love, as Frederick Keener has pointed out, came to have a variety of positive meanings in eighteenth-century moral thought after having reached its lowest ebb among the Puritans of the previous century; and one major effect of this egocentric hedonism was that it supported the idea of the "natural Equality" of human desire.[25]

If Johnson believed in the doctrine of future rewards, he was decidedly at odds with his contemporaries who emphasized the immediate pleasures to be derived from beneficence. To loosen the purse strings of his worldly congregation, Joseph Burroughs, for instance, preached a sermon based an Acts 20:35, "It is more blessed to give than to receive," to the Society

for Relief of the Widows and Orphans of Protestant Dissenting
Ministers (2 March 1742): "Though the receiving a needful
supply, by what means soever it comes, is always attended with
a delight, proportioned to the concern which possessed the
mind before that supply came; yet it is vastly inferior to that
noble pleasure, which attends the mind of the generous benefactor. For it is very much allayed, by the consideration of
being dependent, in many cases, where the person relieved has
as strong a disposition to generosity, as those who relieve
him."[26] Burroughs's voluptuous Latitudinarianism is remote
from that "most ardent Charity" celebrated by Johnson's account of Savage. Even if espousing a belief in a divine distribu-
tion of rewards in the afterlife, Johnson, we have seen, was not
one to applaud the cultivation of the poor for the sake of an
immediate pleasure to be enjoyed from beneficence.

Whatever the danger of "voluntary delusion," Savage's story
is an exposé of a society based on greed and plutocratic power;
and besides inculcating a healthful self-interest as the best
defense, there is another aspect to Johnson's moral thought
that is much less hopeful than the Stoic commonplaces he
usually brought forth, though strangely overlooked in the
most representative commentary. In *Rambler* 166 Johnson
questions whether anyone, gifted or otherwise, born in poverty
can ever attain the self-esteem necessary for harmonious social
interaction. Furthermore, as Johnson premises that Savage
truly believed himself to be the illegitimate son of a nobleman,
he sees that his character's identity problem is all the more
exacerbated under the contemporary system of patronage.

The epigram for this essay, from Martial, establishes at once
the economic determinism of human behavior: "*Pauper eris
semper, si pauper es, Æmiliane, / Dantur opes nullis nunc nisi
divitibus*" ("Once poor, my friend, still poor you must remain, /
The rich alone have all the means of gain").[27] As in Johnson's
poem *London*, the plight of the talented person living in urban
poverty is the main theme; and the aphoristic arguments that
derive inevitable moral and psychological effects from the
socioeconomic condition are devoid of the Stoic consolation
found elsewhere in his writings. Instead, we find ourselves

locked in a master/slave dialectic with only the slightest hope of escape—the hope of some "ardent Charity" for relief.

Johnson's source for the basic argument in *Rambler* 166 appears to be Hobbes's *Leviathan*, chapter 11 of part 1, which concerns the way individuals relate to each other in society. Rejecting the final causality of a summum bonum, Hobbes does not see happiness as the fulfillment of desire but rather as a continual process of restless striving after objects that ends only in death. Assuming that all desire is self-oriented, the value of any social action will depend on the pleasure or pain involved, whether in the doer or in the beneficiary. Of crucial importance in the credit/debit transaction is the social class of giver and receiver as well as the amount given and owed: "To have received from one, to whom we think ourselves equal, greater benefits than there is hope to requite, disposeth to counterfeit love; but really secret hatred; and puts a man into the estate of a desperate debtor, that in declining the sight of his creditor, tacitly wishes him there, where he might never see him more. For benefits oblige, and obligation is thraldom; which is to one's equal, hateful."[28] By contrast, a gift received from one held to be superior allegedly inspires love and gratitude, which may be sufficient recompense to the donor. Likewise, so long as there is the probability of repaying a loan from an equal or inferior, the transaction can be amiable and can even result in mutual benefit. Hobbes does not elaborate the predicament of borrowing from an inferior; Boswell's own report of Johnson's ill humor at being asked to repay him a shilling reflects more on the lender than on the borrower![29]

It is the despair of those who are condemned to indebtedness without respite that is Johnson's theme in *Rambler* 166. In the world that Robert Walpole helped to make, the stigma of being outside the privileged classes determined by birth and fortune is nearly inescapable. Johnson describes the universal predicament of one approaching a patron: "He whose confidence of merit incites him to meet without any apparent sense of inferiority the eyes of those who flattered themselves with their own dignity, is considered as an insolent leveller." Since Johnson admits his own fear of being rejected while petitioning a favor, his sympathy with Savage's "confidence of merit" while begging for support is understandable. On the other hand, "no better success will commonly be found to attend servility and dejection" (*Rambler* 5:117). If Savage, for instance, had tried to be tactfully submissive (as Boswell reports he did after the falling out with Lord Tyrconnel), he would still have felt the other's scorn for not having acted with adequate self-confidence: "A request made with diffidence and timidity is easily denied, because the petitioner himself seems to doubt its fitness" (*Rambler* 5:118). What for Hobbes was only a special case under a benevolent despotism has become for Johnson a century later an intolerable deprivation of selfhood; and Savage's open resentment of his creditors shows a heroic protest against the demeaning condition of poverty: "His Distresses, however afflictive, never dejected him; in his lowest State he wanted not Spirit to assert the natural Dignity of Wit, and was always ready to repress that Insolence which Superiority of Fortune incited, and to trample the Reputation which rose upon any other Basis than that of Merit: He never admitted any gross Familiarities, or submitted to be treated otherwise than as an equal" (99). Johnson surely does not criticize the petitioner's demand for self-respect; and in contrast to Hobbes, who could imagine cheerful acceptance of a benefactor as a superior, neither the biographer nor the hero is inclined to submit to "that Insolence which Superiority of Fortune incited."

At the center of Johnson's essay is a norm hopelessly beyond the reach of the poor: the reciprocal action of giving and receiving among the privileged classes. "There is an affection not arising from gratitude or gross interest, by which similar natures are attracted to each other, without prospect of any other advantage than the pleasure of exchanging sentiments, and the hope of confirming their esteem of themselves by the approbation of each other" (*Rambler* 5:119). But for the poor or socially anonymous, such affection is denied: "By what means can the man please . . . who has no power to confer benefits; whose temper is perhaps vitiated by misery, and whose understanding is impeded by ignorance?" (*Rambler* 5:118).

Furthermore, vulnerability in the credit/debit exchange only invites the sort of aggressive retaliation that Lord Tyrconnel showed his onetime protégé, on the principle Hobbes defined: "To have done more hurt to a man, than he can, or is willing to expiate, inclineth the doer to hate the sufferer. For he must expect revenge, or forgiveness; both of which are hateful."[30] On a similar egoistic basis, Johnson emphasizes the necessity of self-love as a means of withstanding the predator's violence; in being always pleased with himself against all odds, Savage's "noble pride" in spite of his poverty is a necessary defense against the vicious cycle of gift and obligation that results in thraldom and hatred.

Johnson's final point in *Rambler* 166 is to show the interlocking of patronage with subservience, which obstructs the "spontaneous fondness" possible between those who enjoy the freedom of property. In contrast to this happy state among equals, stands the stereotype of "men of eminence followed with all the obsequiousness of dependance"; and the editors of the Yale Edition of *The Rambler* cite one of Johnson's letters with the anecdote of "a man who asked no other favour of Sir Robert Walpole, than that he would bow to him at his levee" (*Rambler* 5:119). The last paragraph of this essay draws the moral inference that "We must learn to separate the real character from extraneous adhesions and casual circumstances" (*Rambler* 5:120); but everything in the previous discussion has virtually ruled out such a possibility—everything, that is, except the "most ardent Charity" exhibited by Savage on that inspired occasion.

JAMES GRAY

Johnson's Portraits
of Charles XII of Sweden

What was it in the character and personality of Charles XII of
Sweden that both attracted and repelled Samuel Johnson?
Was it his peculiar brand of Stoicism, his invincible stubborn-
ness, his extraordinary ability to exact every ounce of loyalty
from his subordinates, his magnanimity towards the vanquished, or his vindictive punishment of an obstinate foe?
Perhaps a combination of these qualities. More particularly,
Charles's almost superhuman courage, his self-effacement, his
piety—his dominant characteristics, in short—were the components that Johnson saw as potential raw materials for a
tragedy or a biography. At a deeper level, the Swedish leader's
much-discussed fatalism, his apparent swing from exemplary
Christian fidelity to an unexplained skepticism, must have
puzzled Johnson, or perhaps reminded him of his own occasional lapses and questionings.

What this essay sets out to do is to examine some hitherto
neglected aspects of Johnson's attempts to portray the character of this enigmatic hero, whose exploits intrigued him as
much as they had inspired Voltaire.

The year of Johnson's birth, 1709, coincided with the year of
the shattering defeat of Charles XII at Pultowa, where the

massive armies of Peter the Great of Russia annihilated the
small but seasoned force of Swedish troops and demolished
the hope of their leader to dominate the whole of eastern
Europe. Forty years later, in *The Vanity of Human Wishes*,
Johnson epitomized the life, career, and character of Swedish
Charles, substituting him for Juvenal's Hannibal, in thirty-two
of his best and most memorable lines.

> On what foundation stands the warrior's pride,
> How just his hopes let Swedish Charles decide;
> A frame of adamant, a soul of fire,
> No dangers fright him, and no labours tire;
> O'er love, o'er fear, extends his wide domain,
> Unconquer'd lord of pleasure and of pain;
> No joys to him pacific scepters yield,
> War sounds the trump, he rushes to the field;
> Behold surrounding kings their pow'r combine,
> And one capitulate, and one resign;
> Peace courts his hand, but spreads her charms in vain;
> "Think nothing gain'd, he cries, till nought remain,
> "On Moscow's walls till Gothic standards fly,
> "And all be mine beneath the polar sky."
> The march begins in military state,
> And nations on his eye suspended wait;
> Stern famine guards the solitary coast,
> And Winter barricades the realms of Frost;
> He comes, not want and cold his course delay;
> Hide, blushing Glory, hide Pultowa's day:
> The vanquish'd hero leaves his broken bands,
> And shews his miseries in distant lands;
> Condemn'd a needy supplicant to wait,
> While ladies interpose, and slaves debate.
> But did not Chance at length her error mend?
> Did no subverted empire mark his end?
> Did rival monarchs give the fatal wound?
> Or hostile millions press him to the ground?
> His fall was destin'd to a barren strand,

A petty fortress, and a dubious hand;
He left the name, at which the world grew pale,
To point a moral, or adorn a tale.[1]

In this compendious yet concise historical sketch, Johnson manages, while hewing fairly close to the Juvenalian line (but without Juvenal's satirical pungency), to include most of the elements that made up the complex character of the Swedish monarch. When a mere boy, Charles led his country in what history was to call the Great Northern War—a conflict that extended from 1700 to 1721, three years beyond Charles's death, and involved all the important nations of Europe at one time or another. Johnson's portrait of Charles is much more favorable than Juvenal's of Hannibal, whose profound hatred of Rome had provoked that satirist's gleeful depiction of a power-hungry tyrant whose rapacity was equalled only by his elephantine oafishness. Charles, by contrast, is presented as physically powerful, spirited, fearless, irrepressible, indefatigable, loved as well as feared, never succumbing to either pleasure or pain, unhappy in peace and most active in war. Most confident when other nations, like Russia and Poland and Denmark, are ranged in alliance against him, Johnson's Charles secures the surrender of one king, Augustus II of Poland, and the resignation of another, Frederick IV of Denmark; but, dissatisfied with a victorious peace, he is determined to push on until he has conquered Russia and the world beyond. Impeded by famine and winter, he is vanquished at Pultowa and driven into exile in Turkey, while his future descends into the hands of Catherine the tsarina and the minions of the Grand Pasha. Then Destiny, rather than military operations or the overturning of his empire, brings about a demise almost as anticlimactic as the poisoning of Hannibal: death by the bullet of an unknown assailant in the small fortress of Frederikshald in Norway. Thus the name of which the world had once stood in awe and fear becomes the subject of fabled history, good enough to provide an object lesson, perhaps, or to embellish a story. Nearly all the sad details are there, encapsuled in Johnson's ruefully satiric lines.[2]

Whether his special interest in Charles XII was first aroused by the coincidence of the events of 1709 or not, there is no doubt that it was well sustained in the years between Johnson's birth and the publication of *The Vanity of Human Wishes*. The meteoric rise and the cataclysmic fall of the Swedish leader captured the imagination and stirred the hearts of a generation for whom the military exploits of Marlborough at Blenheim and Ramillies were a proud and thrilling memory. There had been a spate of writings, with many of which, we may be sure, Johnson had some familiarity, including three books by Defoe,[3] besides numerous references in the periodical press. Johnson's interest in the subject was stimulated most of all by Voltaire's *History of Charles XII, King of Sweden*, first published in French in 1731. Within a year, it had been translated into English by Andrew Henderson and was republished four times within almost the same number of months.[4] As it was Voltaire's first successful historical work, written during or shortly after his exile in England, it enjoyed something of the status of a best seller, continuing in popularity well into the nineteenth century. While Johnson had some reservations about Voltaire's reliability as a historian, we have William Seward's testimony that he thought this particular book "one of the finest pieces of historical writing in any language."[5] Of the other studies of Charles XII that followed Voltaire's celebrated work, the most notable was that of Gustave Adlerfeld, *A Military History of Charles XII, King of Sweden*. It was published in 1740, two years before Johnson announced, to John Taylor, his own intention of writing on the subject. The translation of Adlerfeld's book, from the French, was assisted in part by Henry Fielding.

Fielding, incidentally, has the protagonist of his novel *Amelia*, William Booth, relate to Major Bath the fact that Charles XII, "the great king of Sweden, the bravest and even fiercest of men, shut himself up three whole days in the midst of a campaign, and would see no company, on the death of a favourite sister."[6] The legendary Charles found his way into other novels of the 1740s, including *The Fortunate Foundlings*, by Eliza Haywood (1744), in which one of the foundlings, Horatio, joins the army of the Swedish king, only to be captured by the Russians and imprisoned in St. Petersburg. From the many references to the Duke of Marlborough and the "rampaging and rapacious Charles," it is clear that the interest of readers was still being excited by such episodes.[7]

As late as 1763 we find Lord Chesterfield recommending Charles XII as an example to his rather unadventurous godson. In one of his letters composed in French, after describing "Pierre le Grand" as a man who had, through travel, self-education, and sheer perseverance, achieved greatness despite having come from a barbarous nation, he writes, "Charles douze de Suède qui avait les manières assez grivoises disait que rien n'était impossible à un homme qui avait du courage et de la persévérance." Then he counsels his godson to study Charles XII, as well as Gustavus Adolphus and his daughter Christina, as part of his preparation for a visit to Sweden and Denmark.[8]

Chesterfield's knowledge of Charles XII, like Johnson's, was derived in large part from Voltaire's *History*. In a letter to the French author, dated 27 August 1752, he had praised Voltaire's great talents as a historian, and, perhaps not realizing that a new edition had appeared in 1750, added, "Vous nous avez donné il y a longtemps l'histoire du plus grand Furieux (je vous demande pardon, si je ne peux pas dire du plus grand Héros) de l'Europe."[9] In a letter to his son, written at Bath shortly afterwards, 4 October 1752, he praised Voltaire to the skies. "How delightful is his History of the Northern Brute, the King of Sweden! for I cannot call him a Man; and I should be very sorry to have him pass for a Hero, out of regard to those true Heroes; such as Julius Caesar, Titus, Trajan, and the present King of Prussia [Frederick the Great]; who cultivated and encouraged arts and sciences; whose animal courage was accompanied by the tender and social sentiments of humanity; and who had more pleasure in improving, than in destroying their fellow-creatures."[10]

The apparent ambiguities in Charles's character, the great northern brute with the courage of a lion, capable of trampling upon whole nations and yet vulnerable to great griefs, evi-

dently intrigued Chesterfield as they had fascinated Defoe and
Fielding, and as they would engage the interest of other writers, like Smollett, who produced a later translation of Voltaire's *History* (heavily dependent on that of Henderson). The
same complex of contrarieties, in so many ways reminiscent of
Hannibal, must have challenged Johnson, who recognized the
dramatic potential of Charles's story.

Robert Folkenflik has reminded us that Johnson was drawn,
as a biographer, to those heroes who had been imbued with
Christian stoicism and who had faced sickness, adversity, pain,
trial, and death without complaint, managing to "maintain
their virtues despite their troubles," sustained as they had
been by their piety and characterized, in the words of *The
Vanity of Human Wishes*, by "obedient Passions and a Will
resign'd." More particularly, Folkenflik has noted (as did Paul
Fussell before him) that Johnson was struck by the anticlimactic exits of some of the celebrities of the past. "The death of
great men is not always proportionate to the lustre of their
lives," writes Johnson in his *Life of Pope*. "Hannibal, says Juvenal, did not perish by a javelin or a sword; the slaughters of
Cannae were revenged by a ring. The death of Pope was im-
puted by some of his friends to a silver saucepan, in which it
was his delight to heat potted lampreys." And Folkenflik observes that "this heroic analogue itself is drawn from a satire,
in fact from *the* very portrait on which Johnson's character of
Charles XII . . . is modeled."[11]

There is, of course, much more to Johnson's interest in
Charles. It is clear, for instance, that, for all his abhorrence of
war and his critical attitudes to militarism,[12] he had a lifelong
admiration for the courage and daring of the common soldier.[13] After all, he had grown up in the atmosphere of war. He
had read, in Addison's *Spectator* 139, of the greatness achieved
by commanders such as Marlborough, whose victories in the
War of the Spanish Succession had elevated him to highest
esteem. Lichfield, where Johnson was born, was a military
center, with regiments quartered in the town. Even its cathe-
dral bore scars inflicted by both sides in the Civil War, and it
had its own grim history of carnage dating from the time of the

emperor Diocletian when a thousand Christians were martyred. It was in recalling this episode that George Fox, founder of the Society of Friends, during a visit to the place in 1641, uttered the famous cry, "Woe to the bloody city of Lichfield!" Indeed, Johnson himself gives the derivation of the name of his native town in the *Dictionary* as "the field of the dead . . . so named from the martyred Christians."[14]

On a lighter note, it will be recalled that one of David Garrick's first amateur theatricals in Lichfield was a presentation of Farquhar's *The Recruiting Officer*, a comic portrayal of the activities of the army during Marlborough's wars, for which Johnson was invited to compose a prologue. Garrick's own father was a recruiting officer, and Farquhar himself had recruited soldiers in Lichfield while staying at The George (the scene of another of his plays, *The Beaux' Stratagem*). The part of Captain Plume in *The Recruiting Officer* was modeled on the playwright. The editor of *Biographia Dramatica* describes the epilogue as "a sprightly and martial one, adapted to the successes of the British arms at that glorious period, being introduced by the beat of the drum with the Grenadier-march."[15]

With this background in mind, we should not think it surprising that Johnson found much to admire in the profession of arms. When he expressed his celebrated opinion that "every man thinks meanly of himself for not having been a soldier," for instance, he no doubt meant what he said. The comment that follows this remark is even more interesting, that if Socrates and Charles XII had been together "in any company," Charles would have commanded more respect as a soldier than Socrates as a philosopher. Though Boswell suggests that Johnson may have been caught up here in "the common enthusiasm for splendid renown," he admits that his subject had a special admiration for the Swedish king, not only as a soldier, but as a greatly revered and respected leader.[16] "Fine clothes," said Johnson on one occasion, "are good only as they supply the want of other means of procuring respect. Was Charles the Twelfth, think you, less respected for his coarse blue coat and black stock?" Here, perhaps, he had in mind Charles's meeting with King Augustus of Poland at Guntersdorf in 1707, when he wore jackboots, a piece of black taffeta around his neck in place of a cravat, and a coat of coarse blue cloth, with brass buttons. There was, of course, a sound military reason for his habitually plain dress: it made him a less conspicuous target on the battlefield, and on one occasion, at least, it helped save his life.[17]

So deeply interested was Johnson in the life, character, and exploits of Charles XII that he planned at one time to write either a play or a biographical history about the subject. As has been mentioned, he announced this intention in a letter to his friend, John Taylor of Ashbourne. The letter was dated, conjecturally, by R.W. Chapman as 10 August 1742, and apparently misdated "June" by Johnson or by Taylor. Since seven years would elapse before the publication of *The Vanity of Human Wishes*, with its epitomized portrait of the Swedish monarch, we must infer that Johnson scrapped his plan in the interim or failed to find a publisher for his play or history. He was busily engaged in several important projects for Cave at the time, including a "historical design" of some sort; his *Life of Savage*, which was nearing completion; and miscellaneous pieces on recent European military and diplomatic history. His work on Charles XII may well have been pushed into the background, though one hopes that, like some suspected planet or Saturnian moon, it might yet be discovered.

The fact that Johnson mentions it in the very letter in which he asks Taylor to "keep close" the manuscript of *Irene* strongly suggests that a tragedy along similar lines was already on the drawing board. The passage in question reads as follows: "I propose to get Charles of Sweden ready for the winter, and shall therefore, as I imagine be much engaged for some Months with the Dramatic Writers into whom I have scarcely looked for many years. Keep Irene close, You may send it back at your leisure." In his edition of Johnson's *Letters*, Chapman follows Malone, G.B. Hill, and the editors of the Oxford edition of the *Poems* in voting for a play as against a history, and the context quoted gives support for their preference. The combination of readying the piece, whatever it was, "for the winter"—that is, the winter theatre season—and being "engaged for some Months with the Dramatic Writers," in order, presumably, to shape his material on Charles XII into a play suitable for the stage, seems to point in that direction. Beyond these tantalizing hints we have no letter or other document to corroborate this theory, no communication with Garrick on the subject, and no evidence of any kind to show that a play about Charles XII, by Johnson or by anyone else in England, ever reached the boards.[18]

Whether Garrick would have been interested in such a play is doubtful. He had had enough trouble with *Mahomet and Irene*, to be sure, to make him reluctant to contemplate another imperial tragedy by Johnson.[19] We do know that a friend of Garrick's, Dr. James Stonehouse, suggested the possibility of a play about Patkul, whose torture and execution on the orders of Charles XII had been a much-discussed episode in the checkered career of the Swedish king, and that Stonehouse had recommended Hannah More as the potential playwright, but there is no record of Garrick's response to that overture.[20] It is, nonetheless, worth noting that the infamous treatment of Patkul was considered by Johnson to be as much of a turning point in Charles's career as the humiliating defeat at Pultowa, and the dramatic significance of the king's apparent vindictiveness on that occasion would have been obvious to him.[21] (To sound a facetious note on a rather gruesome subject, the spectacle of Patkul being broken on the wheel, not to mention his subsequent quartering, would have created even greater technical problems for Garrick than the strangulation of Irene with a bowstring, which caused such an uproar at the first night performance of Johnson's play in 1749.)

The Reverend Percival Stockdale (1736-1818), who was a neighbor of Johnson's in Bolt Court, made an observation in his *Memoirs* in this connection (noted, incidentally, by John Wilson Croker, but apparently overlooked by G.B. Hill and L.F. Powell): "Charles the Twelfth was guilty of a deed which will eternally shade the glory of one of the most splendid periods that are presented to us in history—the murder of Patkal [sic].

Dr. Johnson remarked to me, when we were conversing on this tragical subject, that Charles had nine years of good and nine of bad fortune; that his adverse events began soon after the execution of Patkal, and continued to his death. Johnson may be pronounced to have been superstitious; but I own that I was sensibly struck with the force of the observation."[22]

If Stockdale's report is to be relied upon, Johnson would appear to have anticipated, in a certain sense, some findings of the editor of Charles XII's letters, Ernst Carlson, and of his later biographers, one of whom suggests that Charles "seems to have gradually elaborated a theory of alternating cycles of good and bad luck, which he expresses in the words: 'In times of war unlucky events must occasionally happen in order that [future?] luck may have freer course.' "[23]

Whether Charles himself in any way ascribed his military débacles merely to bad luck, however, is debatable. Following the severe defeat at Pultowa, and the surrender of his generals, Lewenhaupt and Creutz, at Perevolotjna shortly afterwards, he went through a period of profound soul-searching during his exile in Turkey, where, as a refugee, he sought asylum from Achmet III, Sultan of the Porte, the Ottoman government at Constantinople. Hence the truth of Johnson's lines:

> The vanquish'd hero leaves his broken bands,
> And shews his miseries in distant lands;
> Condemn'd a needy supplicant to wait,
> While ladies interpose, and slaves debate.

The reference here is to the interposition of the tsarina, later Catherine I, who played a major role in bringing about the peace treaty between the Russians and the Turks on the banks of the Pruth on 1 July 1711, thus denying Charles XII the chance to join forces with the sultan to crush the armies of Peter the Great. During his time in Turkey, moreover, there were frequent power struggles within the seraglio while Charles's future was being discussed. But Johnson's account of this period of frustration omits to mention the debate that must have gone on within the Swedish king's own soul, and leaves the impression that the rest of his career was something of an anticlimax as he became the victim of Chance and Destiny.

In fact, Johnson's string of rhetorical questions leads us into one of the most interesting aspects of Charles's later philosophical position. As Robert Nisbet Bain has noted, the king's religious views in the latter part of his short life (he died in his thirty-seventh year) took on "a strange tinge of fatalism, whereby he tried to explain, to his own satisfaction, the undeserved failure of his righteous cause." Bain also points out that no great military commander ever left more to chance than did Charles XII, "and some military critics have even denied him the capacity of drawing up a complete and regular plan of campaign beforehand. But this is going too far. Klissov and Holowczyn [two of his signal victories] are standing monuments of his generalship. . . ."[24]

A more recent study, by Professor R.M. Hatton, has confirmed the fact that, following the defeat at Pultowa, Charles ascribed his grievous setback to "a fated and unlucky happening" [et öde och olyckligt tilfalle], and has noted that this is the first time that the word "fated" is mentioned in the king's surviving letters. Later, Professor Hatton goes on, "the adjective gave way to the noun when he had, in private letters, to impart the news of the death in battle of individuals known to him. Ödet—Fate with a capital—meets us again and again in the letters of his later years. But whether this sprang from an aversion to link God with sorrows inflicted or from an unwillingness to accept chastisement at God's hands or even from some modification of his religious beliefs we cannot tell."[25]

This emphasis on Ödet gives the concluding lines of Johnson's portrait of Charles XII a special validity, the more remarkable because he was not aware, presumably, of what the king had said in the letters to which Professor Hatton refers. In particular, the arresting lines, "His fall was destin'd to a barren strand, / A petty fortress, and a dubious hand," carry much more weight than the plain fact of history, that Charles was killed by a bullet, or a cannonball, in the Norwegian fortress of Frederikshald in 1718. The words "destin'd" and "dubious" convey both the sense that Fate had indeed played the decisive role and the speculation, still not totally laid to rest, that the king might have died by the hand of an assassin, perhaps even that of his own aide-de-camp, who made what historians now regard as a spurious confession to the deed.

The notion of Fate is, of course, central to the theme of *The Vanity of Human Wishes*, but it is also germane to Johnson's special interest in Charles XII's religious views and convictions. When we recall that Johnson was engaged in his revisions of *Irene* for the stage about the same time as he was composing his poem, Charles's involvement with people of the Moslem faith during his years of exile in Turkey takes on a new importance.

Here it is of some interest to note that Voltaire, in his preface to the 1750 edition of his *History of Charles XII* (a history to which Johnson, as has been shown, was especially indebted), takes issue with those historians who had misrepresented facts and repeated absurdities, and he singles out the story of Mahomet II as an example. "To render this conqueror more hateful, they [the historians] add, that he cut off the head of his mistress to please his janissaries. . . . Consult the real annals of Turkey, compiled by Prince Cantemia, [and] . . . you will see how extravagant it is to imagine that the soldiers should concern themselves with what passes between the sultan and his women, and that an emperor should cut off the head of his favourite to please them. It is thus, however, that the greater part of history is written."[26] Though Voltaire is using this instance to vindicate, by contrast, his own methods of ascertaining the details of Charles XII's career, however astonishing they might appear to the reader, we may wonder whether he was aware that Johnson, in basing his tragedy, *Mahomet and Irene*, very largely on *The Generall Historie of the Turkes* by Richard Knolles, had incorporated the very absurdities mentioned in that preface. In any event, the coincidence is as remarkable, in its way, as that of the nearly simultaneous composition of *Candide* and *Rasselas*.

Voltaire specifically rejects the view that Charles XII had become indifferent to the teachings of the Lutheran church as a result of meetings with Leibnitz in 1707, but he admits that his exposure in Turkey to Mohammedanism and to a variety of other faiths made him less and less enthusiastic about the religion of his fatherland. Quoting the opinion of the Count de Croissy, Voltaire notes that "of all his old principles, Charles retained none but that of absolute predestination, a doctrine that favoured his courage, and justified his temerity."[27]

There seems little doubt that, during his largely self-imposed exile in Turkey, Charles found much to praise in the Moslems' virtues and customs, such as their abstinence from alcohol, their generous laws of hospitality, their patience, and their loyalty to their word of honor. His admiration and tolerance may have been misinterpreted by some of his countrymen as turning back on his own faith, but his own court chaplains, Nordberg and, after 1717, Rhyzelius, testified to his steady devoutness to the end.[28]

Johnson's view of the matter is characteristically different. He believed that Charles, imbued with a fanatical sense of his mission to conquer the world, was equal in ambition only to the tsar of Russia, Peter the Great, himself. In *Adventurer* 99, indeed, he describes Peter and Charles as "the last royal projectors with whom the world has been troubled," and goes on as follows:

Charles, if any judgement may be formed of his designs by his measures and his enquiries, had purposed first to dethrone the Czar, then to lead his army through pathless desarts into China, thence to make his way by the sword through the whole circuit of Asia, and by the conquest of Turkey to unite Sweden with his new dominions: but this mighty project was crushed at Pultowa, and Charles has since been considered a madman by those powers, who sent their ambassadors to sollicit his friendship, and their generals "to learn under him the art of war."

Lest his readers accuse him of an unstinted admiration for the exploits of a military hero like Charles, however, Johnson adds this sobering thought:

> I am far from intending to vindicate the sanguinary projects of heroes and conquerors, and would wish rather to diminish the reputation of their success, than the infamy of their miscarriages: for I cannot conceive, why he that has burnt cities, and wasted nations, and filled the world with horror and desolation, should be more kindly regarded by mankind, than he that died in the rudiments of wickedness; why he that accomplished mischief should be glorious, and he that only endeavoured it should be criminal: I would wish Caesar and Catiline, Xerxes and Alexander, Charles and Peter, huddled together in obscurity or detestation.[29]

Whether it was this desire to "huddle" Charles XII into oblivion at some time between August 1742, the date of the letter to Taylor, and October 1753, the date of *Adventurer* 99, that prevented Johnson from writing his proposed play or history we may never know. What we do know is that, the last quoted assertion notwithstanding, Johnson continued to admire the Swedish monarch, and to be intrigued by his behavior as a military commander, until the closing years of his life. His memorable comparison of the standings of Charles and Socrates in public esteem, for instance, was recorded on 10 April 1778; and in October of the same year, in a letter to Hester Maria Thrale, he saw fit to compare Charles, this time not unfavorably, with Alexander, Darius, Caesar, Pompey, Tamerlane, Bajazet, Peter the Great, and Augustus.[30]

The reasons for this sustained interest in "the great northern brute," to use Chesterfield's phrase for Charles XII, are not hard to find. In the letter just mentioned, Johnson is referring to the sheer toughness of spirit that brought out the best in the great military leaders of the past: their ability to endure hardship and the most miserable of living conditions, to discipline themselves and their men to the farthest extremes of self-

sacrifice, and to encounter the last enemy with "a will resign'd." Of all these shining qualities Charles XII was surely an
exemplar, even if his fabled rapacity for territorial gains, his
burning of cities and wasting of nations, and his one most
shameful act of retributive cruelty, the execution of Patkul,
made him a candidate, in Johnson's eyes, for oblivion or de-
testation.

CATHERINE N. PARKE

Johnson, Imlac, and Biographical Thinking

In the *Life of Dryden* Johnson offers the following image to characterize the author of genius: "He only is the master who keeps the mind in pleasing captivity; whose pages are perused with eagerness, and in hope of new pleasure are perused again; and whose conclusion is perceived with an eye of sorrow, such as the traveller casts upon departing day."[1] The larger Johnsonian territory onto which this image of pleasing captivity opens and for which it serves as a figure is the area of his hope for ongoing education throughout life: for the possibility of associating both learning and teaching with our entire beings, and for the way repetition, return, and recommencement, which are necessary for establishing the varied rhythms of true education, are distinct from the mere repetitiousness that characterizes education gone wrong. Johnson would have readily understood, a century and a half later, Gertrude Stein's version of this crucial distinction between true and false repetition in education. In *Everybody's Autobiography* she gives the name of "school" to education that uses the exercises of false repetition and the mastering of inert facts as its principal activities. For Johnson, as for Stein, such mistaken ideas of learning are dangerous not just to individuals but to an entire culture. And they are dangerous as certainly to the life of the imagination and the ethical life as they are to the life of the intellect.

Johnson was alert to the dangers of false repetition, but he also affirmed the epistemological paradox that books, like the world, answer only questions that we know how to answer or for which we know how to recognize what would constitute an appropriate answer. To learn is to recognize and to repeat what, in some sense, one already knows. The new is always a version of the old and the old of the new. The figure of pleasing captivity dramatizes an ongoing reciprocity of questions and answers that both anticipate and validate one another, on the one hand, but whose relationship is never merely expected and hence never boring, on the other. According to Johnson, the teachers and books that teach us best, like the life best lived, hold us in voluntary thrall to the promise of a newness that will also be familiar. Unlike, for instance, those lessons taught by Prince Rasselas's first tutor in the Happy Valley, which, the prince observes, must be forgotten in order to give pleasure, these lessons are repeatedly and variously interesting. Successful lessons invite us to remember them again and again, but variously, over time. Such a notion of remembering the same lesson differently over time intersects the adjacent issue of the possibility of constructing a present that is accurately, as well as innovatively, connected with our past, and also imaginatively directed toward our future. Such connectedness is, for Johnson, the precondition for creating that most imaginary, illusive, and necessary mode of time: the present.

For Johnson, so this essay proposes, the experience of pleasing captivity in reading is the primary characteristic of all successful education. And it is also his synecdoche for a life well lived. Pleasing captivity assumes a stance of questioning faith in regard to books and to the world. It is a stance that values the creation by individuals alone and in community of an active connection between past and future. Yet more importantly, such a stance encourages our cultivating a healthy resilience toward and even the expectation of pleasure from the experience of differing from or disagreeing with ourselves over time. As we return to old texts and find new pleasures and instruction there, we learn the art of consciously differing from ourselves. And such differing has for us intellectual, ethical, and emotional value. Such an activity is both educational and therapeutic in the way it gives us an opportunity to mock-encounter benignly with that anxious activity of differing from others. And the importance of this exercise lies in the fact that, as Johnson knew so well, the experience of differing from others often inspires fear, suspicion, and anger. By mock-encountering autobiographically with our own differences over time in the drama of our pleasing captivity to literature, we experience difference with relative safety. And this experience gives us, in turn, practice in expecting the best biographically from our differences with others. We may thereby, perhaps, come both to accept those differences charitably and to use them well.

The educational drama of pleasing captivity that, throughout his career, Johnson was interested in defining, and which this essay will examine in *Rasselas* and the *Lives of the Poets*, characteristically unfolds as a series of exchanges and transformations, or "traffick," to use the term associated with the master teacher Imlac. This "traffick" is biographical in nature and structure. To put it another way, this traffick is what we might call "biographical thinking." In *Rasselas* Johnson dramatizes a model of biographical thinking in education whose aim and method are to maintain an ongoing conversation about one's own and other people's lives. The *Lives of the Poets* proposes cumulatively a model of education considered to be a kind of historical conversation, but this time as an exercise in a kind of imaginative excess whose aim is to people the empty present with a full concept of ourselves understood to be conscious inheritors of and participants in a conversation with the past.[2] In each instance it is probability, whose "proofs are always uncertain, to some extent obscure, and always a matter of degree," that accounts for the continuity as well as for the variety of these conversations.[3] The aim of such educational renovation, as Johnson defines it, is to establish a healthy trafficking among past, present, and future that produces in the present moment ideal conversation. This ideal conversation is considered to be both a worthy end in itself and an emblem of the community of love and esteem that constitutes, for Johnson, the ground of our thinking.

To open the discussion of *Rasselas* and the *Lives* let us begin by considering a passage from the *Life of Sir Thomas Browne* that offers a useful perspective on an issue not identical with, but fundamentally related to the matters we have laid out for examination. The passage identifies what Johnson understood to be the distinctive predicament of the gifted person, and it will frame for us the larger problem, which the trafficking between conversation and excess collectively works toward resolving: how to make meaning in the present. Johnson notes in the *Life of Browne* that this author failed to write an account of his early travels. Johnson regrets this failure and takes the occasion to note that the most gifted thinkers often decide not to write, either because they much prefer to collect knowledge than to impart it, or because they find few things "of so much importance as to deserve the notice of the publick."[4] In the first instance, the writer defers writing for the pleasure of collecting. By this deferral he or she overemphasizes the self and underemphasizes the social act of writing. In the second instance, the writer defers writing out of a paralyzing sense of humility, underemphasizing both the self and the social act of writing. Neither motive is a positive or intended evil. And both, ironically, mark the energetic mind of genius that demands more of itself than it does of others. But in each instance nothing is produced, and hence the present is abdicated and left empty. An error has occurred in biographical thinking. And both instances are serious liabilities for the drama of collective creative effort that is the history of our education. The empty present is for Johnson the very type of all moral and philosophical error that, while it may be philosophically high minded, is nonetheless mistaken. The correction of such an error that is based on the refusal to act lies in biography— biography considered here to be not merely a kind of writing, but an attitude of mind and readiness of the imagination to think probabilistically. Biography is, for Johnson, the quintessentially probabilistic genre. "We know somewhat, and we imagine the rest," he writes in the *Life of Roscommon*. And biographical probability is fundamentally an act of the imagination. Accurately directed by probability, biography helps us withstand the temptation to neglect our duty of joining in the conversation of history and thus filling the present usefully.

Johnson understands and uses probability as he understands and uses biography. As biography is for him more than merely a genre, so probability is more than merely a technique of thought. Rather, both are conditions of thinking, models of communication, and ways of living. One might even say, borrowing Heidegger's concept of how language speaks us, that for Johnson probability thinks us and biography lives us. Both give us a constant impetus to place something in the empty present, thereby to assert the meaning of the past in the present moment that is, in turn, directed toward an imagined future. This assertion of meaning constitutes our very identities. Empowered by their operations, we find ourselves able to make the psychologically difficult shift from the pleasures of collecting knowledge to the risky, but necessary and responsible activity of distributing our knowledge according to a rhythm of repetition and recommencement that we understand to characterize true education. Johnson has anticipated such twentieth-century thinkers as Gaston Bachelard in his understanding that whatever lasts longest must begin over and over again well.

Rasselas is an experiment in just such thinking about the educational virtues of beginning over and over again. Here Johnson works out the implications of the image of pleasing captivity in a narrative of recommencements that are never boring.[5] The travelers in *Rasselas* experience many emotions along their journey: hope, discouragement, anger, terror, and suspicion among them. But never as a group are they bored. And for Johnson the absence of boredom is significant. It measures the mental health that has been collectively established by the participants and gives evidence that they have succeeded in creating a rhythm of genuine educational repetition and imaginative vitality. Escaping the dull captivity and

negative education of the Happy Valley, the travelers engage in
a series of pleasing captivities to their several searches and
researches, captivities that are themselves revised and reconsidered along the way. The revisions and reconsiderations take
the form of the self-renewing drama of biographical conversation, as the travelers tell stories about their own and
other people's lives.

Imlac is the master teacher who knows how to traffick in
healthy repetition back and forth over the same routes without
repetitiousness. He operates on an understanding of communication as occurring neither merely in subject matter nor
even in the setting of that subject into the motion of conversation. Rather he understands conversation as a kind of
circuitry or ground for, not simply the subject of, all human
exchanges—for the generation, communication, and continuity of knowledge that constitute our history. Imlac operates in part rationally on a model of induction that counts on
matters of fact to serve as the field for interpretative generalization. But he also, and more critically for the kind of
educational point that Johnson wishes to make, operates imaginatively on a model of knowledge that proposes participation
in a conversation, not merely discovery, as its primary aim.
Such participation, understood to be both a means to and an
end of knowledge, is served especially well by biography.

Throughout *Rasselas*, as Imlac directs traffick in the form of
a round of biographical exchanges, we come to see this drama
as itself constituting the formal significance of the travelers'
journey. It is the pursuit of probabilistic knowledge—of knowing somewhat and imagining the rest—which requires us to
admit that, from time to time, we may come to think differently from ourselves. Such differing from ourselves over
time, which the travelers in *Rasselas* rhythmically experience
through a conversation, is no liability, though it is a measure of
our finiteness. And this finiteness, in turn, argues the travelers'
need fully to inhabit the present by speaking with one another.
One important repetition in the tale that illustrates this drama
of self-differing over time is the episode of the prince deciding
to undertake his own version of Imlac's earlier travels, which

the poet has just recounted, as it combines with Imlac's decision to return to the world with the prince. Rasselas's decision is inspired by Imlac's autobiography, which holds the young man in a pleasing captivity, all the more pleasing to the prince because he is sure that he will succeed where the poet has failed. Imlac's return to the world is inspired by his desire to see, not the world, but the prince seeing the world. So indeed, both travelers live out their own pleasing captivities, each engaging in a distinctive repetition and return, neither performing an original act. And thus each alone (because both together) carries within himself the possibility of healthy difference and renewal in the future, thanks to his having filled the present moment.

Imlac's particular gift as a teacher is his ability to inspire in his students the belief that they can return to his teaching and find there something both new and distinctively their own. When the old is remembered well, it always seems new because such a conversation makes a probable place for the present listener's imaginative participation. To say this is yet another way of saying that the drama of conversational probability takes as its chief aim, not the accurate approximation of words to things, but the continuance of the conversation through the intermediation of biographical thinking. Imlac, as teacher, aims first and foremost to keep conversation going. And this priority requires imagining the listener's mind—its familiarities and its fears. Such a priority requires being especially sensitive to moments when the drama of conversational probability goes off track and also being sufficiently inventive to reimagine it back on course. Imlac so values the educational and emotional value of conversational continuity that he is even willing to swallow his pride to preserve it. At difficult moments, when he is interrupted by his exasperated students who question his accuracy and his motives so that their conversation is seriously jeopardized, Imlac strategically turns the talk in another direction. Nekayah, for instance, makes perhaps the most significant interruption in *Rasselas* when she remarks to her brother that she suspects Imlac's jealousy of their search for the happy choice of life, "lest we should in time find him mistaken."[6] For a student thus to suspect her teacher is serious indeed, since learning must assume trust on both sides, particularly on the side of students who must also be able to believe that their teachers unselfishly wish them well. Where there is no trust, there can be no learning.[7]

Johnson understands such trust to be a precondition for the ongoing conversation of education. Recognizing both the necessity and fragility of such trust, he never takes it for granted. Several times later in the story Johnson shows the students affirming Imlac's teaching as they recognize that it was right after all. These affirmations do not, however, merely prove that Imlac was right. Rather, and more significantly, they dramatize the students' recognition that Imlac has been trustworthy all along. The teacher's trustworthiness, so we come to understand as the tale progresses, is far more crucial to education than his merely being right. For error, unlike untrustworthiness, does not undermine the very structure and assumptions of the activity and thus close off the conversation. If we add to the harmful effects of suspicion the two motives that, as we noted earlier, Johnson identifies as conspiring to keep the gifted writer from writing, we can better take the measure of the importance of ongoing conversation in *Rasselas*. As an active assertion of meaning in the present against the several temptations to silence, conversation is a significant achievement.

Throughout *Rasselas*, then, the concern with subject matter is deemphasized and the concern with keeping open and reliable the circuitry of communication is italicized. Such openness conditions the possibility of healthy repetition. This latter concern becomes the primary aim of the journey. Such an aim is predicted in the familiar opening lines of the tale, which express a monitory aphorism without conclusion, a strategy that invites the possibility of our making repeatedly different interpretations over time. "Ye who listen with credulity to the whispers of fancy, and pursue with eagerness the phantoms of hope; who expect that age will perform the promises of youth, and that deficiencies of the present day will be supplied by the

morrow; attend to the history of Rasselas prince of Abissinia"(1). One might say that the conclusion is implicit in the
syntax and that to express it, one need only insert negatives
into each of the parallel phrases; e.g., age will not perform the
promises of hope, the deficiencies of the present day will not be
supplied by the morrow. But *Rasselas* is more resilient of
meaning, and offers a more pleasing captivity to interpretative
repetition that is not mere redundancy, than such a reductive
reading would suggest. Furthermore, we have for comparison
other aphorisms in the story that do offer explicit conclusions,
such as the maid's comment about the broken cup, "What
cannot be repaired is not to be regretted," or Imlac's observation on choices, that you cannot drink at once from the mouth
and source of the Nile. In the specific way these aphorisms
differ from the formula that opens the tale, we may see how the
opening of the tale makes possible our returning to the tale at
different times and finding there different meanings. *Rasselas*
begins, as it ends, without simple closure. And this repetition
illustrates the educational principle of recommencement and
return and the possibility of differing from ourselves over time
that are, for Johnson, at the heart of true learning.

The recentering of the journey's formal significance in establishing a safe, ongoing conversation in which the participants come, though not without difficulty, to trust one another,
is also anticipated by such details as Rasselas's particular
interest in the European postal system. Among all the various
details in Imlac's account of living in the world, his description
of mail service pleases the prince most. His interest in this
circuitry of information by which distant friends may be
joined offers an image of what Rasselas later will come to insist
upon when he, alone, urges the princess and Pekuah not to
disguise themselves in order to meet the mad astronomer. The
women's intentions are, no doubt, kindly. They want to cure
the astronomer's madness. But Rasselas astutely perceives the
serious error in their plan. " 'I have always considered it as
treason against the great republick of human nature, to make
any man's virtues the means of deceiving him, whether on
great or little occasions. All imposture weakens confidence

and chills benevolence' "(120). Any act that weakens confidence and chills benevolence is a crime against that very community of trust upon which, in turn, the possibility of communication depends.

The measure of success of the travelers' journey turns out to have been their continuing conversation. Such a notion of success occurring in the maintenance and right working of circuitry, rather than in the communication of the message per se, is yet another way of imagining a solution to that pair of problems that Johnson identifies in the *Life of Browne*. Each of those failures to write represents a misunderstanding of the importance of keeping a conversation going. In both instances the writer's mistake is not to write. And in each case this failure is the error of the literalizing imagination, one that cannot see the circuitry for the text. It is ironically true in each case that this failure is the error of an imagination that operates too literally. The several possible blocks that may be experienced by the writer of genius become non-issues when the importance of ongoing conversation is given prominence. Such a reimagining of priorities may, as Rasselas observes, have serious implications for matters of human relations more generally considered. " 'It is our business to consider what beings like us may perform; each labouring for his own happiness, by promoting within his circle, however narrow, the happiness of others.' "(73). Notably absent here is any statement about what might literally or objectively promise happiness. Rasselas here proposes not a substantive view of happiness, but an ideal of a certain kind of action or performance that links and interconnects one's own and other people's happiness. Thinking in terms of circuitry, rather than only of subject matter, has implications for the quality of one's psychological as well as intellectual thinking.

By both emotional and intellectual temperament and inclination Johnson was on the side of Thomas Hooker's concept of the interrelation of all truth: "by long circumduction, from any one truth all truth may be inferred" (*Lives* 3:99). And the drama of the characters' journey in *Rasselas* embodies this idea in ways that, by now, we have begun clearly to see. These figures act out a drama that argues such an interrelation among pleasure, truth, and happiness. From any one of these three truths, the other two may be inferred; not, perhaps, always attained, but always inferred. The episode of the mad astronomer exemplifies this drama of "circumduction" (a leading around or about) toward the truth most fully and complexly. Setting out to find happiness for themselves, the young travelers come to value one another's happiness sufficiently to stop their travels and invent a drama for this unhappy man's recovery. Their fondness for him grows, as does his for them, while they perform this therapeutic drama. And this new exchange of affection has already been anticipated by Imlac's earlier affectionate acquaintance with the astronomer. As the young travelers make a practical outlet for their imagination of happiness, they revise that happiness as an anticipated object into happiness as an improvisatory performance. They work toward imagining a conversation with this lovable, gifted, and troubled figure that is based on truth, gives pleasure, and results in happiness. In this context, Rasselas's insistence that the young women arrange their interview with the astronomer honestly and without recourse to disguise, begins to make obvious sense. For the young women to begin their conversation with a lie would from the outset corrupt the possibility of inferring other truths from a single truth in this, their drama of curiosity and charity.

Happiness, pleasure, and truth are presented in *Rasselas* as a kind of interconnected network of moral improvisation. The travelers invent, as they go along, what would seem to contribute probabilistically to both their individual and collective happiness. Their dramaturgical skills improve as they travel. This drama of invention is based on an understanding of the interrelations of judgment and imagination that cooperate to produce ideal reality. For, as often as vain wishes and dreams are called into question throughout the tale, never is the existence of an ideal reality seriously questioned, nor the possibility of the circumduction of all truth undermined. Toward the end of their journey, Imlac instructs his fellow travelers in an imaginative exercise to validate the ideal reality of thought.

The passage is a familiar one: " 'Consider your own conceptions . . . and the difficulty will be less. You will find substance without extension. An ideal form is no less real than
material bulk: yet an ideal form has no extension. It is no less
certain, when you think on a pyramid, that your mind pos-
sesses the idea of a pyramid, than that the pyramid itself is
standing. . . . As is the effect such is the cause; as thought is,
such is the power that thinks; a power impassive and indiscerptible' "(131–132). By validating the reality of thought, Imlac affirms the reality of the search that the travelers are
making. Although their empirical discoveries take them no
closer to finding an object of real happiness, and thus they
seem to be on a retrograde mission, this objective failure does
not call into question the subjective reality of thought itself. It
does not follow from the fact that some dreams are vain that,
therefore, all unobjectified wishes are unreal. Conceptions
exist as certainly as do material objects. And in this certainty,
this reality, of thought lies its possibility for misuse.

If we grant either conceptual or empirical reality unilateral
power over our imaginations, if we succumb to the fascination
of either alone, we are in danger. Thought is real, and the world
is real. For Johnson, the crucial matter is guarding against
coming so powerfully under the sway of one of these notions
that the other vanishes. But if certainty and stability are two
criteria for happiness, then it also follows that the travelers
need only turn to their thoughts, not to the content of that
thought, but to its impassive and indiscerptible power, which
generates thought, in order to make the happiness they have
not found. And, of course, at this late stage in their journey,
they have been doing precisely this for quite some time. Beginning with the reality of thought, other realities, such as happiness, follow by circumduction.

The concept and, more importantly, the biographical drama
of such circumduction also inform Johnson's writing of the
Lives of the Poets. How precarious yet how necessary for communication are the bonds of trust, how slow such bonds in the
making, how often taken lightly, how indispensable for think-

ing and for creating the present. Hence Johnson's refrain of genealogies, notations of indebtedness, and recitals of inheritance throughout these biographies. Johnson records the names of the teachers of famous writers; he notes who expressed debts to whom, which sons rightly honored their parents, and who among parents lived long enough to enjoy their sons' success. Johnson understands such questions of indebtedness and inheritance to be more than matters simply of historical accuracy or of proper accounting. They are examples of biographical thinking understood to constitute the very condition of possibility for writing history—here in the form of biography—in such a way that it does not seem to be an unhappy burden, but rather an empowering and consoling body of knowledge.

The past, for Johnson, is an object neither of investigation nor of sentiment and nostalgia.[8] It is, rather, a way for humans to project themselves into the present and toward a livable future. To fail to mention the teachers of those to whom we, in turn, owe debts is to commit what Johnson calls in the *Life of Addison* a "historical fraud" whereby we unpeople the past, thus leaving ourselves alone and unconnected with our present as well as with our future and our past. Now Johnson's high valuing of truth is well known. But the way he thinks about truth in relation to the psychological importance of biographical thinking and writing, understood to be a way of living out our history, is worth our special note. If by neglecting to name the teachers of famous men we commit a historical fraud with larger implications for the erosion of our present history, so by naming those teachers we do ourselves, more than we do them, a service. To rehearse our intellectual debts, as Johnson in, for instance, the *Preface to Shakespeare* lists all his editorial predecessors, is to assert a collective historical truth that empowers our current efforts.

All of our inheritances, whether debts or pleasures, are interlinked. And accurately acknowledged pleasure, like accurately acknowledged debt, functions as an important individual and collective cultural resource. An author such as Shakespeare, who has pleased many and pleased long suffi-

ciently to be named an Ancient, is a resource of truth and thus
something on which we can rely. We can, to be sure, rely on him
for the substance of his work, but also, and more importantly,
for the circuit of inheritance to which his generations of readers belong. Hence the reason for Johnson's annoyance at those
critics who, for the sake of mistaken notions about the worth of
originality and fame, would paradoxically question Shakespeare's reputation. It would be hard to think of a less obsequious critic than Johnson, or of one less unwilling to criticize
where criticism is due. But he would have us rightly recognize
Shakespeare to be a national resource and his reputation to be
a collective truth arrived at historically and probabilistically
through many years and many readings. Hence his efforts in
editing Shakespeare's texts become one of the bases of the
culture's collective and ongoing conversation in the present.
For a critic to interfere with Shakespeare's capacity to please
threatens more than our pleasure (although this for Johnson is
no small threat): it threatens the very ground of communication.

Such a sturdy notion of the promise and legitimacy of a
present that is substantially related to the past serves for
Johnson as a healthful preventive of the various errors in
thinking that we almost inevitably commit when we unpeople
our past, notably fantasies of omnipotence that usually result
in attitudinizing melancholy. Fantasies of omnipotence always
end in loneliness, dull thinking, and sedated imaginations. We
need our histories to be excessively crowded and our thanks to
be energetic in order to inspire the good thinking of imaginative gratitude. Johnson does not narrowly measure the implications of omitting thanks. Rather he sees the implication of
such omission for the larger matter of imagining a present and
of earning our inheritance by perceiving that inheritance to be
the foundation of a new project or problem that we take to be
our own.[9] To fail to acknowledge debts is, to be sure, a moral
failure. But Johnson would have us consider more largely how
such a failure is both an epistemological error and a sin
against the possibility of pleasure. To fail to live in the midst of
a many-voiced conversation with the past in the present re-

sults in lives like those of the miserable inhabitants of the Happy Valley who are bored and bitter because they refuse to imagine indebtedness and to recognize difference.

Biography, for Johnson, offers precisely the needed exercise in imaginative excess and difference needed to counteract such dangers. By imagining others, we empower ourselves to use the present well. Such is the use, for example, of trying to imagine the state of English criticism before Dryden wrote his *Essay of Dramatic Poesy,* a work whose assumptions have so informed the grounds of subsequent thinking about literature that we have difficulty imagining a time before his critical principles existed. To neglect giving Dryden his due is not a mere clerical error, but a serious error of the biographical imagination. It is symptomatic of a kind of epistemological autism which, in turn, denies us access to the true power of our imaginations. By acknowledging in detail and by actively thinking through our inheritance from Dryden and other poets, we prepare ourselves both substantively and psychologically to undertake our own projects in the present. Such exercise is, in Johnson's eyes, the chief use of biography. While the theme of *Rasselas* is the importance, difficulties, and rewards of keeping a conversation going among different people, the theme of the *Lives of the Poets* is the use and pleasure of that many-voiced drama of reading that constitutes our literary history—a drama in which we may differ from one another and even from ourselves over time. Johnson recognizes that, for instance, all of his readers may not be equally interested in the cancels of Pope's *Iliad,* so he brings his examples to a close before he personally might wish to. He admits that he, as critic, ages; that he forgets, becomes bored, may fail to finish what he begins. Throughout he emphasizes that his readers' first responsibility is to the author in question, not to him the critic. And he endorses the reader's right to differ with him.

The perception and valuing of difference, which is to say the capacity to imagine that there was a time before Dryden had established the first principles of English criticism, or that all readers may not find Pope's cancels equally fascinating, weighs heavily in Johnson's canon of critical principles as an exercise for cultivating educational alertness and preventing habit from dulling how we think and imagine. The *Lives of the Poets* is a series of exercises in biographical alertness, as Johnson brings into view aspects of his writers' work, life, creative intelligence, and reception that sometimes border on invisibility. Other examples include his mention of Richard Savage's jailer, whose kindness in circumstances of conventional brutality and hardheartedness is an imaginative act of goodness, which Johnson thinks deserves special note; of the unnamed woman relative who deserves mention because of her kindness to Savage "in opposition to influence, precept, and example" (*Lives* 2:337); and of Richard Steele, about whose remarkable love for his more gifted friend, Addison, Johnson comments, "It is not hard to love those from whom nothing can be feared, and Addison never considered Steele as a rival; but Steele lived, as he confesses, under an habitual subjection to the predominating genius of Addison, whom he always mentioned with reverence, and treated with obsequiousness" (*Lives* 2:81). Here Johnson identifies how loving another more talented than oneself gives evidence of a generous imagination, one that can invent emotional possibilities beyond narrow self-interest or envy. And the instance of Addison and Steele's friendship is a notable instance of the interconversion of wisdom, charity, and imagination succeeding against the odds of habit and worldly inertia. Like Dryden's act of the critical imagination in *An Essay of Dramatic Poesy*, Steele's friendship for Addison epitomizes the distinctive operations of the creative mind. And for us, as readers of biography, to observe and consider such acts of the imagination exercises within us their special possibilities. Johnson would have us cultivate a perpetual readiness of the intellect, imagination, and heart to perceive things variously over time, to differ from ourselves, and thus to retain our ability to recognize acts of genius wherever they may occur.

Such pliancy and inventiveness of the moral imagination, its capacity to perceive and think through other modes of thought and action than those already familiar, bear significantly upon the act of criticism. They also bear upon the

psychological and epistemological issue of the relation between reason and emotion in criticism. In the *Life of Pope*
Johnson acknowledges his preference for Dryden over Pope
thus: "and if the reader should suspect me, as I suspect myself,
of some partial fondness for the memory of Dryden, let him not
too hastily condemn me; for meditation and enquiry may,
perhaps, shew him the reasonableness of my determination"
(*Lives* 3:223). The oxymoron that juxtaposes the critic's
"reasonableness" and his "partial fondness" expresses a characteristically Johnsonian truth about the nature of literature
and literary judgments. Critical judgments about literature
depend not primarily upon rules, but upon experience and
comparison. And in such matters "judgment is always in some
degree subject to affection" (*Lives* 2:47). Such fondness
adopted as a critical principle is reasonable because it follows
plausibly from the nature of literature and thus accurately
prescribes the operations of criticism. Johnson does not apologize for his partial fondness for Dryden. Indeed he argues its
reasonableness on grounds that this preference for Dryden is
neither a contradiction of reason nor an attempt to coerce the
reader into agreement. Rather it is the reasonable outcome of
probabilistic reasoning. This outcome further justifies itself
by serving as an invitation to readers to make critical determination based upon their own partial fondness.

This matter of the relationship between reason and
fondness, probability and affection, is related to another larger
issue of how to determine truth. If Johnson has rightly earned
the reputation for scrupulously upholding truth and accuracy,
he does not deserve this reputation for being merely scru-
pulous. The correction of falsehood and improbability in the
Lives of the Poets aims not merely toward accuracy narrowly
conceived, but toward drafting a more comprehensive and
compelling vision of truth as a cultural and historical necessity. Repeatedly in the *Lives* he examines accounts of situations
where dishonesty, falsehood, or hypocrisy seem to have occurred to see whether those circumstances can be explained in
another way. In reviewing the case, he sometimes revises the
findings, as, for instance, in the *Life of Halifax*: "To charge all

unmerited praise with the guilt of flattery, and to suppose the encomiast always knows and feels the falsehood of his assertions, is surely to discover great ignorance of human nature and human life" (*Lives*, 2:47). The passage is astute in its critique of unimaginative and hence unrealistic faultfinding. He insists by implication on the responsibility that those who attempt to imagine other people's motives from external evidence must bring to that project. Their imaginations must be capacious and nuanced. And their sense of the truth that biographical thinking takes as its aim must be as confident as it is complex.

Johnson makes a similar analysis of unimaginative and mistaken faultfinding in the *Life of Pope*. "To charge those favourable representations, which men give of their own minds, with the guilt of hypocritical falsehood, would shew more severity than knowledge. The writer commonly believes himself. Almost every man's thoughts, while they are general, are right; and most hearts are pure while temptation is away" (*Lives*, 3:207-208). Here, as throughout the *Lives*, Johnson makes a gentle, yet searching analysis of the drama of error in human life. We err when we mistake our untested strength for actual strength. But always to call such error hypocritical falsehood will probably compound the error by introducing a new one. That our thoughts and positions, while general, are usually right and our hearts, while untried, are usually pure are truths dependent upon circumstances. When these circumstances change, when we specify our thoughts and test our hearts, the truth no longer obtains precisely as it did before. And so it is not only charitable, but philosophically just to give each other the benefit of the doubt as Johnson does here on the subject of Dryden's being charged with false magnificence:

> We do not always know our own motives. I am not certain whether it was not rather the difficulty which he found in exhibiting the genuine operations of the heart than a servile submission to an injudicious audience that filled his plays with false magnificence. It was necessary to fix attention; and the mind can be captivated only by

recollection or by curiosity; by reviving natural sentiments or impressing new appearances of things: sentences were readier at his call than images; he could more
easily fill the ear with some splendid novelty than
awaken those ideas that slumber in the heart. [*Lives*
1:458-459]

Johnson examines Dryden's so-called "false magnificence"
and finds it to be neither simply an aesthetic error nor
pomposity, but rather the result of his great natural aptitude
for thought overbalancing his lesser gift for evoking feeling.
This analysis serves as more than just an occasion to think
about Dryden. It opens out onto the psychology of invention, of
reading, and onto a general truth pertinent to us all: "We do
not always know our own motives." Johnson shifts and adds to
the originating perspective of the question. And this movement both enriches the possibilities for the kinds of answers
that the question can yield and insures the questioner against
narrow censoriousness. An analysis of error that is truly
worthwhile may be accomplished by bringing to the task a
largeness and subtlety of mind that move us into a newly
conceived imaginative space beyond the boundaries of that to
which the simple critique of error would condemn us.
    Johnson's capacity to shift perspectives, thereby reviewing
the origins of error, constitutes a philosophy that is based
fundamentally on a kind of forgiveness considered to be the
basis of reliable thinking. He would agree with Montaigne that
"the soul is served usefully by error." But he would specify in
addition that the soul may be rightly directed only by forgiveness, understood to be the kind of empathetic inventiveness
and ability to imagine more than one explanation for error—a
capacity that we have observed in the several foregoing examples. Johnson's advocacy of charity as a philosophical principle that supports truth takes its distinctive strength and purpose from the significant odds against which it must con-
tend—odds defined by Johnson's perception of how often people lie, how difficult it is to detect lying, and how pervasive its
harmful effects. He observes in the *Life of Congreve* that

"nobody can live long without knowing that falsehoods of convenience or vanity, falsehoods from which no evil immediately visible ensues, except the general degradation of human testimony, are very lightly uttered, and once uttered are sullenly supported" (*Lives* 2:213). Falsehoods of vanity or convenience erode the very basis of reliable communication and as such are crimes against society.

Johnson recognizes, however, that it is important to distinguish between the conscious lie and human weakness. To imagine ourselves to be strong enough to withstand temptation when we are not currently being tempted may be wrong, but if such imagining is not conscious duplicity, it will come in the course of experience to be naturally tested. And this testing will either confirm or correct what we have imagined. To experience the different force of temptation imagined and temptation actually felt not only humbles us, but more importantly, gives us an adequately complex perspective on how our strengths differ in different circumstances.[10] Such a gain is both moral and philosophical. But when lies lightly uttered and sullenly supported undermine the inherited collective strength of human testimony that is the basis of history and culture, the loss is serious.

The capacities of the imagination both to keep a conversation going, which Johnson examines in *Rasselas*, and to acknowledge debts and conceive things to have been in the past or to be in the future other than they are in the present, which is a focal interest in the *Lives of the Poets*, take center stage again in *A Journey to the Western Islands of Scotland*. It is the biography of a culture and the autobiography of a traveler in that culture. The *Journey* invites our brief consideration as a way of thinking back over the territory we have surveyed. The main problem initially for Johnson in the Hebrides is how to get accurate information from the inhabitants. Often he does not. As Johnson's focus during the travels shifts from trying to get accurate information to trying to understand why he is being given false and contradictory information, a philosophical inquiry develops that differs from the one he had started out with. Although he does remain interested in gathering accurate information about the inhabitants' lives, he becomes increasingly and finally encompassingly interested in understanding the logic that generates their "false" accounts.

The larger issue here at stake is the issue of representation: the power that we grant to language to speak our world. As the journey unfolds, Johnson becomes less interested in rigidly and narrowly questioning Highland information in terms alien to it. Like Imlac, he prefers a conversation to an inquisition. He attempts to discover the logic of the accounts he hears and the system that generates the performance of those accounts in a way that anticipates, for example, his attempt to understand in the *Life of Cowley* the informing logic of metaphysical poetry. How would people come to write such poetry and why? And why would the inhabitants of the Hebrides tell the kinds of stories they tell? As the journey in *Rasselas* begins as an empirical inquiry and develops into a therapeutic and epistemological investigation, so on this tour of the Hebrides the traveler reimagines his investigative givens and priorities. The act of the imagination that can suspend its own givens, as Johnson temporarily suspends his legislative categories of truth and falsehood in order to imagine another organization of mind, bears a family resemblance to the imaginative capacity that we noted throughout the *Lives of the Poets* rightly to acknowledge debts and to invent virtuous acts that are without circumstantial precedent.

The productions of such an imagination are always as startling as they are brilliant and renewing. Their spectacle holds us in a pleasing captivity to the hopeful possibility of renovating history, which is to say, the possibility of living meaningfully in the present by adopting and adapting our inheritances into a set of questions and concerns distinctively and biographically our own. When we read the lives of those who, whether they have made a signal contribution to English criticism, like Dryden, or have been kind to a prisoner, like Savage's jailer, or have valued the conversation of education more than their own egos, like Imlac, we see examples of those who have imagined alternatives to the pattern of dulling habit. The imaginative alternatives that such figures instance ex- emplify a principle of genius that Johnson was always alert to identify in literature and in life—a principle that accounts for how, throughout our lives, by relying upon biographical think- ing and the pleasures of accurate repetition, we continue re- peatedly to learn.

STEPHEN FIX

The Contexts and Motives of Johnson's *Life of Milton*

Edgy. Petulant. Defensive. Contentious. Antagonistic. Critics of Samuel Johnson have often turned to these words when discussing the tone and substance of his *Life of Milton*. Such words do indeed aptly describe the rhetoric of Johnson's argument at certain points; but at what target is the rhetoric aimed? From Johnson's time to our own, readers have been quick to deduce from Johnson's aggressiveness that his primary purpose was to attack Milton's character, and to lower the level of critical esteem Milton's works enjoyed. But the first of these views of Johnson's motives, I wish to argue, has been overstated, and the second is simply mistaken. By attending carefully to what Johnson himself reveals in the *Life* about his purposes as a critic and biographer of Milton, we can discover that Johnson's antagonistic stance is a necessary and integral part of his effort to secure Milton's reputation on more solid and durable foundations.

In many important ways, Johnson likes and admires Milton, a man whose literary efforts, like his own, were strenuous and independent. In his prologue for *Comus*, Johnson praises the integrity of Milton, "Whose gen'rous zeal, unbought by flatt'ring rhymes, / Shames the mean pensions of Augustan times."[1] Years later, Johnson echoes this praise in the eloquent conclusion to the *Life of Milton*. "From his contemporaries he neither courted nor received support; there is in his writing nothing by which the pride of other authors might be gratified or favour gained, no exchange of praise nor solicitation of support. His great works were performed under discountenance and in blindness, but difficulties vanished at his touch; he was born for whatever is arduous."[2]

Yet the popular and critical memory has more often retained the sense not of these and similar laudatory comments, but rather of Johnson's several vituperative, abusive remarks concerning Milton's character.[3] His comments on Milton's blindness provide one memorable example. Though in the passage quoted above Johnson writes with sympathetic admiration for the achievement of the blind Milton, elsewhere he is more harsh and abrupt. Johnson devotes only a brief summary sentence to one of the most important facts about Milton's life: "He had now been blind for some years" (116). Johnson nowhere speculates on the personal anguish blindness must have caused the poet, and with unusual insensitivity, he toys with the imagery of blindness, derisively alluding to Milton as "the one-eyed monarch of the blind" (138). He says that, at the time of the Restoration, Milton, the political writer, was reduced to "kicking when he could strike no longer" (126)—a harsh image exploiting the random imprecision with which a blind man confronts the world.

Comments of this kind are scattered throughout the biographical section of the *Life of Milton*, but, significantly, they arise almost always in discussions of Milton's politics, and only rarely at other times. These attacks are real, but their purpose is limited: to discredit Milton's political views and activities. Johnson explains by implication his lack of sympathy for the blind Milton when he attacks Milton's ingratitude for being included in the King's Act of Oblivion after the Restoration. "For no sooner is [Milton] safe than he finds himself in danger, 'fallen on evil days and evil tongues, and with darkness and with danger compass'd round' [*Paradise Lost*, 7:25]. This darkness, had his eyes been better employed, had undoubtedly deserved compassion; but to add the mention of danger was ungrateful and unjust" (140). Milton's loss of sight was also a loss of power to oppose what Johnson regarded as a just and regular government, and for this reason he manifests little sympathy. The personal attacks are meant to stigmatize the political opinions. Johnson continues, "Of 'evil tongues' for Milton to complain required impudence at least equal to his other powers—Milton, whose warmest advocates must allow that he never spared any asperity of reproach or brutality of insolence" (140). When he is thinking of Milton as a political figure, Johnson can come only to this kind of conclusion.

Yet earlier in the *Life*, when political considerations are not coloring his discussion of Milton's character, Johnson takes pains to present an instance of Milton sparing asperity and insolence, even in a case where he may have had the right to manifest both. Johnson approvingly quotes Edward Phillips, surely one of Milton's "warmest advocates," about the moment when Milton's wife begged permission to return home. "He resisted her intreaties for a while; 'but partly,' says Philips, 'his own generous nature, more inclinable to reconciliation than to perseverance in anger or revenge, and partly the strong inter-cession of friends on both sides, soon brought him to an act of oblivion and a firm league of peace' " (107). When politics is at issue, Johnson finds Milton insolently ungrateful for one act of oblivion; when it is not, Johnson, along with Phillips, finds Milton capable not only of appreciating the virtue of such a generous act, but of performing it himself. Johnson even adds to Phillips's story some flattering details that accord to the republican Milton a surprising degree of political tolerance and generosity: "Milton afterwards received her father and her brothers in his own house, when they were distressed, with other Royalists. . . . He had taken a larger house in Barbican for the reception of scholars, but the numerous relations of his wife, to whom he generously granted refuge for a while, oc-cupied his rooms" (107, 108–9).

Though Johnson has some other reservations about Milton's character that are not exclusively political in nature, politics nonetheless remains the touchstone for Johnson's presentation of them. Johnson connects Milton's republicanism with his "sullen desire of independence," his "severe and arbitrary" management of the home, and his "Turkish contempt of females, as subordinate and inferior beings" (157). As he gloats over the irony of all this, Johnson once again concentrates his doubts about Milton into an observation on his political character: "They who most loudly clamour for liberty do not most liberally grant it" (157).

Significantly, only in those parts of the *Life* where Milton's political character is at issue does any real antipathy for Milton appear; it is absent, for the most part, from the rest of the *Life*, and from Johnson's other oral and written comments on Milton. Johnson makes clear that such remarks are to be understood in a political context; he provides us the means of controlling the implications and limiting the damage of his derisive comments. Moreover, Johnson declines some easy opportunities to extend his objections against the man into his commentary on Milton's art. When writing about *Paradise Lost*, for instance, Johnson—unlike the more sympathetic Romantics—studiously avoids suggesting that this "acrimonious and surly republican" (156) with a "sullen desire of independence" was especially well suited to imagine and create the rebellious Satan.

In assessing the reasons for the antagonistic tone of the *Life*, then, it is important to see the context and limits of Johnson's charges against Milton. It is important too that such charges be balanced against the less vivid, but not less substantial praise Johnson gives to Milton for being, among other things, a loyal son, a religiously devout man, and a writer whose "desire of independence" at least insures his originality and integrity.[4]

We must seek, then, an explanation more comprehensive and satisfying than "personal dislike" or "political prejudice" for the antagonistic tone of the *Life of Milton*. In doing so, it is interesting first to note the ways in which Johnson depicts himself as a critic and biographer of Milton. In the *Life of Milton*, more than in any other biography Johnson wrote, readers may detect the voice of a narrative personality speaking to an audience. Johnson seems here to be unusually conscious of his relation to his own audience, and the tone of his occasional snide remarks suggests his eagerness to ingratiate himself with—or at least to impress—his readers. For example, "All [Milton's] wives were virgins, for he has declared that he thought it gross and indelicate to be a second husband: upon what other principles his choice was made cannot now be known" (131); and "His last poetical offspring [*Paradise Regained*] was his favourite. . . . Milton, however it happened, had this prejudice, and had it to himself" (147).

Though there is, in the voice behind these words, a certain amused bravura, Johnson's eagerness to inject a sense of his own personality and to bring the reader close to him on genial terms may suggest something of the wariness and anxiety he feels in undertaking this project. The *Life* opens on a reluctant note: "The Life of Milton has been already written in so many forms and with such minute enquiry that I might perhaps more properly have contented myself with the addition of a few notes to Mr. Fenton's elegant Abridgement, but that a new narrative was thought necessary to the uniformity of this edition" (84).

Johnson's hesitations are to some extent informed by his sense of Milton's own powerful reputation as a writer, and by the uncomfortable knowledge that at times he will become an adversary by challenging the validity of Milton's technique and vision. Johnson therefore takes the unusual step of invoking the authority of other writers to help support his own views. When he objects in the *Life* to Milton's alleged preference for "physiological learning," Johnson proclaims, "If I have Milton against me I have Socrates on my side" (100). In opening his series of *Rambler* essays on Milton's versification, Johnson goes on at some length about the similarity of his project to Addison's, and assures readers that he is only continuing and expanding a project begun—and legitimized—by his popular predecessor.[5] When Johnson begins his second essay in the series, he cites a quotation from Quintilian praising stylistic inquiries of the kind Johnson is attempting, and then he adds, "Confirmed and animated by this illustrious precedent, I shall continue my inquiries into Milton's art of versification."[6] And at the end of the *Rambler* essay in which he invokes conventional rules of style to show that Milton deviates "from the established practice," Johnson indicates that he is consciously engaged in a struggle. "Where the senses are to judge, authority is not necessary, the ear is sufficient to detect dissonance, nor should I have sought auxiliaries on such an occasion against any name but that of Milton."[7]

Johnson's edginess is a compliment to the power of Milton's achievement and example; his greatness as a writer, which Johnson constantly acknowledges, makes the project of criticizing him difficult and worrisome. But such greatness is not the only source of Johnson's concern, as is evident from one of the metaphors he adopts for his relationship with his own audience and with Milton. Johnson opens his *Rambler* essays on *Samson Agonistes*, in which he challenges prevailing notions of the poem's greatness by arguing that it is badly structured and incomplete, with these words:

> It is common, says Bacon, to desire the end without enduring the means. Every member of society feels and acknowledges the necessity of detecting crimes, yet scarce any degree of virtue or reputation is able to secure an *informer* [my emphasis] from public hatred. The learned world has always admitted the usefulness of critical disquisitions, yet he that attempts to show, however modestly, the failures of a celebrated writer, shall surely irritate his admirers, and incur the imputation of envy, captiousness, and malignity.
>
> With this danger full in my view, I shall proceed to examine the sentiments of Milton's tragedy. . . .[8]

Johnson's self-descriptive image of the "informer" is partly a confident expression of his willingness to expose some of Milton's literary crimes. But it finally reveals less about Johnson's relation to Milton than about his attitude toward other critics, and about the contemporary state of Milton criticism. Immediately above these paragraphs, Johnson places an epigraph which he himself apparently composed: "What doating bigot to his faults so blind, / As not to grant me this, can Milton find?" Johnson's defensiveness and anxiety, and the style that accompanies them, must result partly from his perception of how unfashionable he will seem in objecting to aspects of the poetry and character of such an admired writer. The epigraph, of course, jibes again at Milton, who in his blindness can "find" nothing; but its rhetorical force is now aimed not at the blind Milton, but at his enthusiastic critics, whose blind praise of Milton amounts to "doating," and whose uncritical prejudice in his favor amounts to bigotry.

Against such blind bigotry Johnson is to stand as an informer. But Johnson knows how easy it will be for readers to mistake his motives, especially if they are so unaccustomed to hearing critics speak of any faults in Milton's poetry that they cannot appreciate the constructive nature of such an effort, and cannot place even modest objections in the context of greater praise. Johnson hints that unthinking allegiance to the value of Milton's writing has made suspect any attempt to deal with that writing critically. In the context of such widespread and perhaps unthinking devotion to Milton, Johnson implies, the informer himself risks becoming the criminal.

Like the content of the critical remarks we will examine shortly, Johnson's own self-portrait suggests that his purpose is to respond to, and to correct, what he regards as excessive, unselective, and uncritical praise for Milton from contemporary critics and biographers. This is not to say that Johnson's occasional nastiness and vituperation are something other than what they appear to be, or that they are simply part of a disingenuous rhetorical strategy that overstates the case against Milton in order to counterbalance overstatements in his favor. Surely Johnson's impatience with such overstatements made the tone and content of his argument more contentious. But that contentiousness, I wish to argue, is largely connected with the project of rescuing Milton from the misplaced and misinformed enthusiasm of his admirers, and of articulating the standards upon which Milton's strongest case for fame as an artist may be built.

Some initial evidence for this claim may be found by returning to Johnson's two essays on *Samson Agonistes*. The first
essay opens, as we have seen, with the image of the critic as
informer. After explaining which aspects of the poem are
worthy and unworthy of praise, Johnson gains the confidence—in himself and in his audience—to change his self-
descriptive metaphor. He imagines himself no longer as an
informer, but now as a gardener whose critical shears at once
bring violence and life to the flowers. "Such are the faults and
such the beauties of *Samson Agonistes*, which I have shown
with no other purpose than to promote the knowledge of true
criticism. The everlasting verdure of Milton's laurels has nothing to fear from the blasts of malignity; nor can my effort
attempt to produce any other effect, than to strengthen their
shoots by lopping their luxuriance."[9]

Significantly, Johnson chooses this more positive metaphor
at the *end* of his critical examination of Milton; the carefulness
of his criticism has earned him, he must think, the right to a
more agreeable image. It is also significant that Johnson does
not dispute Milton's claim to greatness; his greatness, Johnson
indicates, is what makes this project legitimate and necessary.
This gardener intends to make a new kind of case for Milton's
greatness, one that he expects will ultimately enhance, not
diminish, the poet's reputation. He seeks to do so in several
ways: by responding to those who had praised Milton more
exuberantly than any poet could afford to be praised; by suggesting that Milton's reputation needed to be based less on
legend and enthusiasm, and more on scholarship and discriminating taste; and by focusing attention on those poems of
Milton, such as *Paradise Lost*, that justify the poet's claim to
greatness, and shifting attention away from those, such as
Lycidas, that for Johnson do not.

There had been many biographies of Milton before Johnson
wrote his in 1779, and several editions. Among biographies the
most significant were those by John Aubrey, John Phillips,
Anthony à Wood, Edward Phillips, John Toland, and Jonathan
Richardson; and the most significant edition, a variorum in-

cluding a new life of the poet, was that by Bishop Thomas Newton in 1749.[10] Joseph Addison, to whose series of *Spectator* essays on Milton Johnson acknowledges his own indebtedness in the *Rambler*, "made Milton," Johnson says, "an universal favourite, with whom readers of every class think it necessary to be pleased."[11] Lesser critics and biographers took up the cause, and Milton's praises were soon being sung by "every class" in society.[12]

It is against the portrait emerging from this tradition of enthusiastic attention to Milton that Johnson defines himself. As we read the *Life*, gradually we become aware that Johnson is engaged in a struggle with earlier biographers and critics of Milton. That Johnson's eye is trained on his predecessors is apparent from the frequency of such phrases as these: "*He is supposed* about this time to have written his Arcades" (93); "*It is told* that in the art of education he performed wonders" (99); "His widow . . . is *said to have reported* that he lost two thousand pounds" (153) (my emphases). In many instances where he seems to be parodying Milton, Johnson really is questioning the reliability and judgment of his biographers. For instance, what may at first appear to be a slighting remark about Milton is more likely an attack on Newton's unqualified report of the poet's extensive reading. "When he left the university he returned to his father, then residing at Horton in Buckinghamshire, with whom he lived five years; in which time he is said to have read all the Greek and Latin writers. With what limitations this universality is to be understood who shall inform us?" (91). Certainly not these enthusiastic partisans of Milton, Johnson thinks.

He apparently believes that earlier biographers focused undue attention on the least important aspects of Milton's life and achievement. He finds them pedantic for inquiring why Milton selected a new publisher for *Paradise Regained* and *Samson Agonistes*. "Why a writer changed his bookseller a hundred years ago I am far from hoping to discover" (146). He chides earlier writers for their careless claims about Milton's elision of vowels. "This licence, though now disused in English poetry, was practiced by our old writers, and is allowed in many other languages ancient and modern, and therefore the critics on *Paradise Lost* have, *without much deliberation*, commended Milton for continuing it" (my emphasis).[13] Johnson thinks that even such critics as Addison and Bentley, who examined in detail Milton's style and language, distorted his real achievement. "Addison himself has been so unsuccessful in enumerating the words with which Milton has enriched our language, as perhaps not to have named one of which Milton was the author: and Bentley has yet more unhappily praised him as the introducer of those elisions into English poetry, which had been used from the first essays of versification among us, and which Milton was indeed the last that practiced."[14]

Throughout his writing Johnson makes clear that such careless and credulous praise is destructive not only to the aims of criticism and biography, but also, Johnson thinks, to the legitimacy and stability of the poet's reputation. In no case does Johnson find this problem to be more acute, or its consequences more vexing, than in Milton's. "We have had too many honey-suckle lives of Milton," Johnson reportedly told Edward Malone; and Johnson resolved that his "should be in another strain."[15] Johnson's only other recorded use of the word "honey-suckle" recalls his self-descriptive image of the pruner who saves the tree from strangulation: "I do not . . . envy a fellow one of those honey-suckle wives for my part, as they are but creepers at best, and commonly destroy the tree they so tenderly cling about."[16] In opposing other critics and biographers, then, Johnson's purpose is to protect Milton from the dangers of obsequious and excessive praise.

Perhaps for Johnson the most prominent of these "honey-suckle lives" was that by Jonathan Richardson, whose notes to *Paradise Lost* and life of the poet, published in 1734, enjoyed widespread popularity. Johnson, who mentions Richardson frequently in his own *Life of Milton*, calls him "the fondest of [Milton's] admirers" (134). He deals with Richardson with the same impatient tone noted earlier. For instance, though Phillips and Toland report that Milton composed *Paradise Lost* in erratic spurts, and left off composing for long periods,

Richardson, says Johnson, "conceives it impossible that 'such a work should be suspended for six months, or for one. It may go on faster or slower, but it must go on.' By what necessity it must continually go on, and why it might not be laid aside and resumed, it is not easy to discover" (136).

Richardson's assumptions and ambitions lead him, Johnson thinks, to produce a biography whose tone and content are rhapsodically enthusiastic. Richardson's deepest implication, which must have dismayed Johnson, is that the blinding radiance of Milton's greatness should silence the objections of critics, and make biographers genuflect in reverence. Richardson declines no opportunity to justify, explain, excuse, and ameliorate the behavior of Milton or the defects of his poems. Several selections from Richardson's biography, which in tone and argument closely parallels other works of eighteenth-century criticism on Milton, suggest how deeply sentiment ran in Milton's favor, and how that sentiment shaped— Johnson might say, limited—critical attitudes.

Whatever spots, or blemishes appear upon his judgment in certain points, let the charitable eye look beyond those to his immaculate integrity.

. . . He appears to be studious, grave, chaste, temperate, to be void of covetousness, ambition, or ostentation; . . . to be irreproachable as to any wilful and corrupt deviations, however he may have been mistaken. . . . Above all, his mind shines with noble sentiments of religion, and piety: Lastly, it is truly poetical. Great, strong, elegant, and sublime; it raises and beautifies all its objects as much as Humanity can, and where that fails, has gone farther than any other humane intellect ever attained to.[17]

As enthusiastic as Richardson was, not everyone found him enthusiastic enough. Critics and readers throughout the eighteenth century continued to raise the ante in their discussion of Milton. So perhaps the sharpest difference between

Johnson's view of Milton and the views of his contemporaries may be seen in the work of a biographer who comes after Johnson, rather than before him. William Hayley's *Life of Milton*, published in 1793, is regarded as the first of the "romantic" biographies of Milton; but since it summarizes so well most eighteenth-century views of the poet, it may also be regarded as the culmination of the tradition against which Johnson was defining himself.[18] Though Hayley's work is an eloquent response to Johnson's *Life of Milton*, it is, ironically, full of the very language and arguments that prompted Johnson to write the *Life* as he did.

Because of Johnson's attacks on Milton, Hayley finds himself obliged in his *Life* "to speak rather in the tone of an advocate, than of a common biographer."[19] Advocacy, at least of an uninformed sort, was for Johnson precisely the problem with contemporary criticism of Milton; and the effort to make belief in Milton's poetic greatness virtually an issue of faith is at least as pronounced in Hayley's as in earlier biographies. Calling Johnson Milton's "virulent antagonist," Hayley writes, "I have felt, I confess, . . . resentment in perusing the various sarcasms of the austere critic [Johnson] against the object of my poetical idolatry. . . ."[20] Hayley then wastes no time in elaborating the implications of his own diction:

> Milton, a poet of the most powerful, and, perhaps, the most independent mind that was ever given to a mere mortal . . .

> His poetry flowed from the scripture, as if his unparalleled poetic powers had been expressly given him by Heaven.

> . . . If poetic powers may ever deserve to be regarded as heavenly inspiration, such undoubtedly were those of Milton, and the use to which he applied them was worthy of the fountain whence they flowed.[21]

Like his predecessors, Hayley believes such greatness—itself beyond a critic's challenge—always has its enemies. "It seems as if the good angel of this extraordinary poet had determined that his poetical renown should pass (like his virtue and his genius) through trials most wonderfully adapted to give it lustre; and hence (as imagination at least may please itself in supposing) hence might such enemies be combined against him, as the world, perhaps, never saw before in a similar confederacy."[22] Hayley raises to a heavenly level the struggle for Milton's poetic supremacy and literary vindication, and by implication he registers Johnson in the devil's party.

Inevitably, then, Johnson seems—and is—somewhat defensive about the project he undertakes in the *Life* and in his other commentary on Milton. Johnson is working in a critical atmosphere in which Milton's "immaculate integrity" is confidently opposed to any objections that might be raised about him or about his work, and, what is still more vexing, in which even intelligent readers like Richardson and Hayley can suggest that unfavorable criticism of Milton and his works might be regarded as unfair, unpatriotic, perhaps unchristian. Indeed, even Johnson's careful attention to the technique and style of Milton's poetry runs counter to the prevailing practice and spirit, not only in the detail and explicitness of its critical argument, but also in focusing attention on Milton as a *human* poet—inspired, perhaps, by a muse or by God, but faced like any other poet with the task of making lines scan, similes hold together, and dramatic scenes cohere. So even if everything Johnson wants to say about Milton were favorable, his methods and concerns are bound to challenge the prevailing view of Milton in a way that seems—and ultimately is—antagonistic. But the antagonism is directed as much toward his predecessors in criticism and biography, as toward Milton himself.

Johnson's discomfort with the eighteenth century's lavish praise for Milton should not be taken as evidence of his desire to diminish Milton's stature as a poet, for he consistently opposes all kinds of hyperbolic praise as antithetical to the aims of biography and criticism. The purpose of both is, Johnson thinks, to "improve opinion into knowledge."[23] The more excessive praise becomes, the more nearly biography approaches panegyric, the less likely it is that a critic and audience will attain that knowledge. And for Johnson the danger is, again, not only to the critic or reader, but also to the artist. "Whenever there is exaggerated praise," he says, "every body is set against a character. They are provoked to attack it."[24] Because hyperbolic praise distorts the real value of a man's achievement, and exposes him needlessly to objections that can easily become more vehement than they deserve to be, Johnson thinks that the task of a critic of Milton, particularly in Johnson's time, is to "strengthen the shoots" of Milton's reputation by "lopping their luxuriance."

How does Johnson do this? Certainly not by being grudging or particularly restrained in his own praise for Milton. No other poet, says Johnson in the *Life*, "ever soared so high or sustained his flight so long" (187). "Whatever be his subject [Milton] never fails to fill the imagination" (178). In *Paradise Lost*, "a book of universal knowledge," "every line breathes sanctity of thought and purity of manners" (183, 179). In Milton's works alone, Johnson claims, one finds "a full display of the united force of study and genius" (183). *Paradise Lost* is "a poem which, considered with respect to design, may claim the first place, and with respect to performance the second, among the productions of the human mind" (170).

Johnson's claims for Milton's greatness are not less dramatic or sweeping than those of his contemporaries, but they are the result of a more detailed critical examination of Milton's life and works. Johnson's critique of *Paradise Lost*, for instance, is the longest single discussion of any poem in Johnson's criticism; in it, Johnson—unlike many contemporaries—tries to specify the strengths and weaknesses he sees in the poem, and thereby persuade us of the validity of his claims to its greatness. Johnson's method suggests his belief that criticism of Milton must become less fondly rhapsodic, and more critically substantive, more patient and scholarly. A consideration of how and why he pursues these goals in the *Life of Milton* is best prefaced by a brief review of Johnson's involvement with a man named William Lauder.[25]

The controversy created by Lauder, and Johnson's role in it, need not be detailed here, but the essential facts can be quickly summarized. Between 1747 and 1750, first in the *Gentleman's Magazine* and then in book form, Lauder published a series of increasingly strident claims that Milton had plagiarized large parts of *Paradise Lost*, primarily from the works of such modern European Latinists as Masenius and Grotius. Lauder ultimately claimed that Milton's muse "appears to have been no other, than a library well stored with poetical authors."[26] Lauder was promptly and vehemently denounced; at least ten books and pamphlets, in addition to forty articles in a single magazine alone, disputed his charges.[27] These responses suggest not only the degree of the eighteenth century's enthusiasm for Milton, but its kind as well. Even in the face of the gravest charges of plagiarism, and suggestions that *Paradise Lost* was little better than a patchwork of scenes and images skillfully stolen from other poems, for a long while no one actually examined the original texts that Lauder was, by his own admission, citing only selectively. Critics were too busy insisting that the charges couldn't be true to inquire whether they in fact were false. Had they looked, they would have found what the Reverend John Douglas, casually passing time in the Oxford libraries in 1750, eventually discovered: Milton was no plagiarist, but Lauder was a forger and fraud. He had interpolated into his "sources" passages from a Latin translation of *Paradise Lost*, and then claimed to have discovered the originals from which Milton had "copied the poem." Having sized up the state of Milton criticism in the eighteenth century, Lauder was confident enough to think he could get away with his scheme.[28]

In 1747, Lauder had persuaded Johnson to write an advertisement recommending an edition he was preparing of Grotius, one of Johnson's favorite Latin authors, and the author of one of the poems Lauder would later claim as a source for *Paradise Lost*. Johnson's connections with Lauder have often been taken as evidence of his desire to deprecate Milton. Even one of Johnson's friendly contemporary biographers, Joseph Towers, writes that Johnson's "aversion to Milton's politics, was the cause of that alacrity, with which he joined with

Lauder, in his infamous attack" on Milton.[29] But the evidence now is fairly clear that at the time Johnson knew nothing of Lauder's ultimate claims or fraudulent intentions, and believed—as his own words show—that he was endorsing a worthy scholarly project. He was as surprised as everyone when the fraud was exposed. He confronted Lauder, insisted that he apologize, and helped him write a public confession.

In endorsing Lauder's edition of Grotius in 1747, Johnson especially recommended Grotius' play, *Adamus Exsul*, which, he said, "may be justly supposed the embryo" of *Paradise Lost*.[30] Discovering the "embryo" of Milton's great poem, Johnson stressed, would only enhance a reasoned admiration for Milton's originality and greatness. In the case of *Paradise Lost*, Johnson wrote, no critical project is

> more worthy of rational curiosity, than a retrospection of the progress of this mighty genius in the construction of his work, a view of the fabric gradually rising, perhaps from small beginnings, till its foundation rests in the centre, and its turrets sparkle in the skies; to trace back the structure thro' all its variations to the simplicity of its first plan, to find what was first projected, whence the scheme was taken, how it was improved, by what assistance it was executed, and from what stores the materials were collected; whether its founder dug them from the quarries of nature, or demolished other buildings to embellish his own.[31]

Some thirty years later, echoing this belief in the *Life of Milton*, Johnson again uses the language of gestation. About "some sketches of poetical projects left in manuscript" by Milton at Cambridge (121), Johnson writes, "These are very imperfect rudiments of *Paradise Lost*, but it is pleasant to see great works in their seminal state pregnant with latent possibilities of excellence; nor could there be any more delightful entertainment than to trace their gradual growth and expansion, and to observe how they are sometimes suddenly advanced by accidental hints, and sometimes slowly improved by steady meditation" (124).

Johnson's language consistently suggests that Milton improved upon his sources so decisively, so skillfully, that the discovery of any "assistance" by which *Paradise Lost* "was executed" could only redound to Milton's credit. Rather than thinking that Lauder's discoveries would disgrace Milton, Johnson expected that they would serve the same purpose he intended his own commentary on Milton to serve. To adjust the popular understanding of Milton's achievement so that it would be founded upon an intimate understanding of the way in which a human writer selects his materials, makes literary choices, and improves upon earlier works and examples, was a goal Johnson had set for himself, and one that he thought he shared with Lauder. That Johnson believes the partisans of Milton lacked such an understanding, and had become uncritically enthusiastic, is evident from his opening words in the advertisement to the Grotius edition.

> It is now more than half a century since the *Paradise Lost*, having broke through the cloud with which the unpopularity of its author for a time obscured it, has attracted the general admiration of mankind, who have endeavored to compensate the error of their first neglect by lavish praises, and boundless veneration. There seems to have arisen a contest among men of genius and literature, who should most advance his honour, or best distinguish his beauties. Some have revised editions, other have published commentaries, and all have endeavored to make their particular studies in some degree subservient to this general emulation.[32]

Something more solid, Johnson implies, is needed, if Milton's true greatness as a writer is to be understood and properly appreciated.

These are the contexts and motives for all of Johnson's commentary on Milton, including the *Rambler* essays dis-

cussed earlier, and especially the *Life of Milton*. For these
reasons Johnson is eager in the *Life* to battle biographers and
critics whose rhapsodic and overly dramatic praise was turning Milton into myth or legend; and to remind readers—who,
Johnson thinks, may well have been encouraged by Richardson and others to forget the fact—that Milton was merely a
man, merely a writer. For instance, though Johnson, like earlier biographers, carefully registers the names of Milton's various homes, he is wary enough of the implications of doing so to
mention his anxiety explicitly. "I cannot but remark a kind of
respect, perhaps unconsciously, paid to this great man by his
biographers: every house in which he resided is historically
mentioned, as if it were an injury to neglect naming any place
that he honoured by his presence" (127). The problem for
Johnson is that these biographers were treating Milton's
homes not merely as places made interesting by the poet's
connection with them, but rather as shrines sanctified by his
presence. The biographers of Milton, who regularly confessed
to "idolatry," were worshiping a secular saint, as though they
believed the man who wrote prophetic literature must himself
be regarded as a holy prophet.[33]

Johnson consistently challenges the lore that had grown up
around the legend. He objects to the special pleading of
Milton's biographers as both unnecessary and degrading to
Milton. For instance, Johnson twice complains in the *Life*
about the treatment given by other biographers to Milton's
career as a school teacher.

This is the period of his life from which all his biographers seem inclined to shrink. They are unwilling that
Milton should be degraded to a schoolmaster; but, since
it cannot be denied that he taught boys, one finds that he
taught for nothing, and another that his motive was only
zeal for the propagation of learning and virtue; and *all tell
what they do not know to be true* [my emphasis], only to
excuse an act which no wise man will consider as in itself
disgraceful. His father was alive, his allowance was not

ample, and he supplied its deficiencies by an honest and useful employment. [98]

Here and elsewhere, Johnson—himself once a teacher—finds it necessary to defend Milton against the extenuations of his admirers, who are too eager to remove their hero from the mainstream of life. On this score, the worst offender is Phillips, who insists that Milton educated the children of special friends only, and anxiously stresses that Milton "never set up for a publick school to teach all the young fry of the parish" (109). To this Johnson responds, "Thus laboriously does his nephew extenuate what cannot be denied, and what might be confessed without disgrace. Milton was not a man who could become mean by a mean employment. This, however, his warmest friends seem not to have found; they therefore shift and palliate" (109).

Johnson questions also the unique significance, and sometimes the authenticity, of many inherited stories about Milton. He doubts Newton's assertion that Milton read all the Greek and Latin writers (91). He insists that common sense (and his own experience as a teacher) renders suspicious Phillips's report of the feats accomplished in Milton's small school. "It is told that in the art of education he performed wonders, and a formidable list is given of the authors, Greek and Latin, that were read in Aldersgate-street by youth between ten and fifteen or sixteen years of age. Those who tell or receive these stories should consider that nobody can be taught faster than he can learn. The speed of the horseman must be limited by the power of his horse" (99).

Johnson suggests that Richardson's story about Milton languishing unproductively for hours, and then suddenly bursting forth with a torrent of lines for his daughter to record, is romantically overstated, and that it glorifies and makes unique to Milton a common aspect of the creative process.

These bursts of light and involutions of darkness, these transient and involuntary excursions and retrocessions of invention, having some appearance of deviation from the common train of Nature, are eagerly caught by the lovers of a wonder. Yet something of this inequality happens to every man in every mode of exertion, manual or mental. . . . By Mr. Richardson's relation casually conveyed much regard cannot be claimed. . . .

The story of reducing his exuberance has been told of other authors, and, though doubtless true of every fertile and copious mind, seems to have been gratuitously transferred to Milton.

What he has told us, *and we cannot now know more* [my emphasis], is that he composed much of his poem in the night and morning. [139]

Johnson is impatient with all such stories, for they tend to make Milton's life seem overly dramatic, unusual, pathetic, perhaps even superhuman.[34] The accumulation and repetition of such stories made hyperbolic praise of Milton possible, desirable, and even necessary; and made reliable judgments about his character and poems particularly difficult. Johnson thought that "veneration" for Milton was discouraging just and objective evaluations of his actions. "Let not our veneration for Milton forbid us to look with some degree of merriment on great promises and small performance, on the man who hastens home because his countrymen are contending for their liberty, and, when he reaches the scene of action, vapours away his patriotism in a private boarding school. This is the period of his life from which all his biographers seem inclined to shrink" (98). It is significant that Johnson does not deny that Milton deserves to be venerated. Indeed, elsewhere in the *Life of Milton* he speaks approvingly of the "veneration of his abilities" (130) that protected Milton from prosecution at the Restoration, and he speaks also of the "multiplicity of attainments and extent of comprehension that entitle this great author to our veneration" (147). Precisely because Milton deserves such veneration, Johnson insists that the facts of his life require no extenuation.

I have been arguing that Johnson sought in several ways to reestablish Milton's reputation on firmer foundations: by challenging what he regarded as excessive enthusiasm for the poet; by insisting that Milton be remembered as a human poet, and not as a legend; and by demanding more rigorous critical examination of Milton's work to promote the literary knowledge that would make Milton's reputation secure. I wish now finally to suggest that Johnson, in writing the *Life of Milton*, had two additional goals related to all these: first, to prevent general admiration for Milton from unduly influencing judgments about the literary merits of particular works; and second, to adjust public perceptions of the relative value of poems within Milton's canon so that his reputation might be based upon what Johnson regarded as his strongest work.

Johnson believed Milton's reputation had risen so high that it was increasingly difficult to make independent, discriminating judgments about the value of particular poems. The problem is exemplified, Johnson thinks, by *Lycidas*. "Such is the power of reputation justly acquired that its blaze drives away the eye from nice examination. Surely no man could have fancied that he read 'Lycidas' with pleasure had he not known its author" (165). The same is true of *Samson Agonistes*, which Johnson had demonstrated (to his own satisfaction at least) to be defective as a drama because it lacks a well-structured middle section. Though the defect, Johnson thinks, is obvious, the play remains popular merely because Milton wrote it. "It is only by a blind confidence in the reputation of Milton that a drama can be praised in which the intermediate parts have neither cause nor consequence, neither hasten nor retard the catastrophe" (189); "This is the tragedy which ignorance has admired, and bigotry applauded."[35] And Johnson is careful to say that such distortions do not always work in the poet's favor. Indeed, in the case of *Paradise Regained*, says Johnson, the poem "has been too much depreciated": "Had this poem been written, not by Milton but by some imitator, it would have claimed and received universal praise" (188).

Johnson believes that critics and common readers must carefully consider the individual merits of particular poems; this is the method and message of the *Life of Milton*. Both are related, of course, to Johnson's more significant preoccupation in the *Life*: to identify which poems within Milton's canon are most worthy of praise, and most likely to justify claims for Milton's greatness. One reason this goal must have been particularly important to Johnson was that Milton himself seemed unable to estimate justly the relative value of his various works. Milton did not, Johnson thinks, attach sufficiently low value to his juvenalia: "For his earlier pieces he seems to have had a degree of fondness not very laudable" (161). Johnson's similar belief that Milton thought more highly of *Paradise Regained* than of *Paradise Lost* provoked the parodic response quoted earlier: "Milton, however it happened, had this prejudice, and had it to himself" (147).

But for Johnson there was no question at all about which of Milton's poems was the greatest, and which was to be of primary concern in his own criticism. Johnson praised no poem more generously or at greater length than *Paradise Lost*. There is an abrupt break in the tone and substance of the *Life of Milton* when Johnson turns from Milton's lesser works to an examination of *Paradise Lost*. "Those little pieces may be dispatched without much anxiety; a greater work calls for greater care" (170). And Johnson indeed lavishes such care on the poem; he devotes approximately ten times as much space to *Paradise Lost* in the *Life* as to the study of *Lycidas*, for instance, and approximately twice as much space to *Paradise Lost* alone as to the critical examination of all Milton's other poems. Such measurements only confirm quantitatively what any careful reading of the *Life of Milton* will show: that focusing critical attention on *Paradise Lost* is Johnson's overriding concern.

In the eighteenth century, however, enormous interest had been stirred in such "little pieces" as *L'Allegro*, *Il Penseroso*, and *Lycidas*. Thomas Warton's edition of Milton's minor poems was enjoying enormous popularity. Such prominent critics as Elijah Fenton and Joseph Warton concurred that had Milton "left no other monuments of his genius" than these short poems, "his name" would nonetheless have "been immortal."[36]

Johnson sensed that critics, though acknowledging the greatness and even the superiority of *Paradise Lost*, had come more or less to regard Milton's other works as of equal value, and worthy of equally lavish praise. Though Johnson himself admits that "it was not to be supposed that the writer of *Paradise Lost* could *ever* [my emphasis], write without great effusions of fancy and exalted precepts of wisdom" (188), he believes it is dangerous to regard Milton's works as being equally good. Johnson therefore stresses the theme of inequality in the *Life of Milton*. Though many of Milton's poems are "lusciously elegant," "they are not all of equal value," he says (161). Within *Paradise Lost* itself Johnson sees this imbalance, and does not think it unnatural. "All the parts are not equal. . . . It is no more to be required that wit should always be blazing than that the sun should always stand at noon" (187). Even in his biographical account Johnson carefully elaborates on this theme, as when he scoffs at the wonderment excited by stories that Milton's compositional abilities were uneven. "Something of this inequality happens to every man in every mode of exertion, manual or mental" (139).

This concept of inequality of compositions is a useful lever for Johnson. He is trying to send the minor poems into an orbit free of *Paradise Lost*'s reflected light, where they may blaze or fade according to their own luminosity. So long as the "little pieces" are treated as major satellites of *Paradise Lost*, the force of the epic's excellence naturally will prevail, and all Milton's poems will be judged in light of the brilliant achievement *Paradise Lost* represents. This can have two effects, both of them, Johnson believes, unhealthy: either readers will uncritically transfer their appreciation of *Paradise Lost* to poems much less deserving of praise, or they will reject uncritically those lesser poems because they do not measure up to the standards of *Paradise Lost*.

The extent to which such concerns shape the *Life of Milton* is illustrated again by Johnson's commentary on *Lycidas*, the purpose of which is evident from its context in the *Life*, and the intensity of which is a result of Johnson's desire, traced throughout this essay, to correct public and critical tastes. Here are several of the most important statements that precede and introduce the criticism of *Lycidas:*

The English poems, though they make no promise of
Paradise Lost, have this evidence of genius, that they have
a cast original and unborrowed. But their peculiarity is
not excellence.

That in the early parts of his life he wrote with much
care appears from his manuscripts, happily preserved at
Cambridge, in which many of his smaller works are found
as they were first written, with the subsequent correc-
tions. Such reliques shew how excellence is acquired.

Those who admire the beauties of this great poet sometimes force their own judgment into false approbation of
his little pieces, and prevail upon themselves to think that
admirable which is only singular. [162–63]

Only then does Johnson write what would become one of the
most famous sentences in his criticism: "One of the poems on
which much praise has been bestowed is 'Lycidas'; of which
the diction is harsh, the rhymes uncertain, and the numbers
unpleasing" (163). After reciting for several paragraphs his
objections to the poem, Johnson concludes with a statement,
quoted earlier, whose metaphorical implications serve again
to remind us of the blind, uncritical enthusiasm of Milton's
other admirers. "Such is the power of reputation justly acquired that its blaze drives away the eye from nice examination. Surely no man could have fancied that he read 'Lycidas'
with pleasure had he not known its author" (165).

Johnson wants to keep in perspective the reader's interest in
the "little pieces"—of which *Lycidas* may stand as a prime
example. As he writes in the *Life of Philips*, "Little things are
not valued but when they are done by those who can do
greater."[37] Johnson believes that the minor poems are interesting (as Lauder's Grotius edition was interesting) primarily
because they show the earliest forms of Milton's development,
and remind us of the distance he had yet to travel before
writing *Paradise Lost*. In these early poems there is not even a
"promise of *Paradise Lost*," so they do not deserve to share in
the reflected glory of that poem. But they are not entirely

without interest to Johnson either. They show the early efforts and struggles of the mind that would produce the great epic; that is why Johnson can say that the manuscripts of Milton's early poems are "*happily* preserved at Cambridge" (my emphasis)—not because the manuscripts preserve great poems, but rather because they are "reliques" (of a writer, not a saint) that "shew how excellence is acquired." The minor poems are of interest to Johnson only for the reason Lauder's project was initially interesting to him: they show the foundations, not always secure, of *Paradise Lost*.

The lavish praise *Lycidas* had achieved as a poem in its own right was distorting the perspective on Milton's achievement that Johnson sought to establish. The prominent critic Robert Thyer, calling *Lycidas* a superb poem, abruptly concludes that "the particular beauties of this charming pastoral *are too striking to need much descanting upon*" (my emphasis).[38] Such a judgment must have confirmed Johnson's suspicion that Milton's works were enjoying uncritical praise. Still worse, Johnson must have thought, was that appreciation of the beauties of *Lycidas* had become a decisive standard of poetic taste and literary competence. No less a critic than Joseph Warton proclaimed, "Addison says, that he who desires to know whether he has a true taste for history or not, should consider, whether he is pleased with Livy's manner of telling a story; so, perhaps it may be said, that he who wishes to know whether he has a true taste for poetry or not, should consider whether he is highly delighted or not with the perusal of Milton's 'Lycidas.' "[39] Warton, of course, did not think that *Lycidas* was a greater poem than *Paradise Lost;* but to make *Lycidas* a standard of poetic taste when the public, Johnson thought, had to be shown ways of understanding the superiority of a very different poem, *Paradise Lost*, was surely to mislead and, from Johnson's viewpoint, to disserve the purposes of critical efforts that seek to improve opinion into knowledge.[40]

By studying Milton's poems in relation to each other, and by adjusting popular perceptions of their relative merits, Johnson hoped to describe more precisely what it was that Milton excelled in, and where he was deficient. When he says disapprovingly that *Lycidas* is "one of the poems on which much praise has been bestowed," but *Comus* is a poem "worthy of all the admiration with which the votaries have received it"; when he says that *Paradise Regained* "has been too much depreciated" and that *Samson Agonistes* "has in requital been too much admired"—Johnson in all these cases is again doing what we have throughout this essay seen him do: challenging prevailing notions of what Milton can be praised for most justly and reliably.

Johnson does not wish to lower the popular critical estimate of Milton; he wishes, rather, to make Milton's reputation more durable and persuasive by challenging the "blind confidence" and uncritical enthusiasm that were blurring distinctions among Milton's individual works, and encouraging in readers a kind of "veneration" that made his poems seem "too striking to need much descanting upon." A sentence in a *Rambler* essay begins, "Among those whose reputation is exhausted in a short time by its own luxuriance, are the writers. . . ."[41] Johnson hopes, I believe, to protect Milton's reputation from such exhaustion by the critical act of strengthening its shoots and lopping its luxuriance. To better serve and preserve the poet's reputation, Johnson seeks through the *Life* to impose some order on Milton's flourishing poetic garden—to keep those who tour it on the proper path, and to trim the shrubbery that might obscure our vision of its central tree. His purpose, ultimately, is to prune Milton's garden, not uproot it.

WILLIAM R. SIEBENSCHUH

Johnson's *Lives* and Modern Students

Modern students get little or no exposure to Johnson in high school or in college introductory courses, but it was not always thus. As the countless English and American school editions of *Rasselas* and *Macaulay's Johnson* eloquently attest, for well over a hundred years after his death Johnson was something of an institution in secondary school curricula. Simplified, stereotyped, with selective emphasis given to the moral dimension of his work, vivified indelibly (and many would argue inaccurately) by Boswell, Johnson used to be part of the common imagination to a degree scarcely approximated by any comparable literary figure, living or dead.

It was, in retrospect, a mixed blessing. For, his major works increasingly unread but the phrase, "Sir," on everyone's lips, he may be said to have achieved something like the status of a great poem. He did not have to mean; he only had to "be," and with entirely predictable results. The countless nineteenth-century "coffee table" and gift editions of *Rasselas* and the *Lives of the Poets* notwithstanding, we all know what Becky Sharp thought about the honor of receiving a copy of Johnson's *Dictionary* from Miss Pinkerton, and we all know what she did with it when she got it. And at least we may imagine that Becky knew who Johnson was. I believe the majority of today's college freshmen would be hard pressed to place Johnson in the right century or to make as unsubtle a distinction as that between Sam and Ben.

There are more than a few ironies here. For, English and American scholars have spent much time and tremendously valuable effort since about the 1940s attempting to save Johnson from precisely this sort of entombment in his own celebrity. They have attacked Macaulay's biases and distortions, filled many gaps in Boswell's portrait and perceptions, and steadily redirected scholars to Johnson's own writings.[1] Yet during roughly this same period of reassessment and re-vivification of Johnson within the scholarly community, Johnson began to be removed once and for all from his pedestal in secondary school curricula—at least in America. At the same time that he became better known to modern scholars, he was becoming less and less a monument that secondary school teachers felt obliged to visit, less and less an indispensable part of the steadily dwindling traditional course offerings in colleges and universities in the early and mid seventies (the aftermath of the late sixties). In this country, among people now under twenty-five, I think it is fair to say that Johnson has temporarily ceased to have even a faint resemblance to the status in the common imagination—and even the visual recognition and simplified stereotypic resonance—he once had. As a broad generalization I think it is even fair to say that among those of that age group Johnson has little or no place in the imagination at all.

Obviously, there are two ways of looking at anything. To a pessimistic, traditionalistic, Tory-minded son of Squire Western, the situation might argue the end of civilization itself: Art after art goes out, and all is night. I am far more optimistic. All but the most timeless authors cease to please many and please long because times and values change and the authors seem to have less to say to a new generation than they once did. As I shall suggest, though something like this may have happened to Johnson, the times they are a-changin' once again. And although modern students may be less automatically (and uncritically) predisposed to assume Johnson's importance, they are also suddenly in a position to approach his writing without bias or controlled perceptions. They can read his best work without an oppressive sense of what they are supposed to see or praise. A severe test for a "classic," one might argue, but I believe that, viewed thus, Johnson's writing may once again have some immediate—and not just historical—appeal to students. Not Boswell's or Macaulay's Johnson, but Johnson's Johnson. Not their parents' or grandparents' version, but their own. I shall argue, therefore, that it is time to reexpose high school and beginning college students to Johnson by permitting them to encounter substantial samples of his best prose in introductory and survey courses. And along with the other obvious candidates for inclusion in such courses—the *Preface to Shakespeare*, the *Preface to the Dictionary* and, for the stout of heart, *Rasselas*—I suggest the *Lives of the Poets:* not for their historical importance or as attractive samples of Johnson's prose valued independently of its content or context, but because of the inherent modern appeal of the critical and intellectual acts Johnson performs in them.

Why the lives? Among other things, because they are so quintessentially Johnsonian. Their subject is both human conduct and literary performance. As such, they are a forum for Johnson's literary, social, and moral analysis and judgment. Like other critical and/or moral writings of Johnson's, they imply a comprehensive vision of the world, a way of apprehending and controlling both aesthetic and social experience. They imply—indeed, announce—specific standards by which both texts and men may be read and judged. They afford some of the best and most sustained evidence of Johnson as a practical critic in action. And yet, having said all this, it might seem logical instead to argue that all of these facts might be the lives' most obvious liability.

"Johnson had," said T.S. Eliot, "a positive point of view which is not ours; a point of view which needs a vigorous effort of the imagination to understand."[2] Eliot made this statement in 1944, and it is hard to deny its apparent justness. One does not, after all, have to know a hawk from a handsaw to know that presumably Johnson's critical and moral vision—his most fundamental assumptions and values—has not been fully shared for a hundred years, if not longer. Johnson saw the function of literature as mimetic—far more literally so than we with our broader and more catholic modern tastes can comfortably accept. (One has only to imagine, for instance, Johnson's reaction to Pound, or Baudelaire, or the theatre of the absurd; to cubist painting or *The Waste Land*.) "Great thoughts are always general," said Johnson in the *Life of Cowley*.[3] Yet for over a century we have been far more ready—as a culture—to applaud the artist who has dared to number the streaks of the tulip and express highly personal visions. It is equally clear that Johnson's preference for the general over the particular, for the abstract over the concrete, and his assumptions of unchanging moral, social, and aesthetic values are preferences and assumptions that have not been commonly shared for most of our century. "The foundation of bourgeois statement of fact," said Roland Barthes—a distinctly modern voice—"is *common sense* when it stops on the arbitrary order of him who speaks it."[4] Common sense has for some time been a slightly patronizing term used to characterize Johnson's thinking and, though neither Johnson nor his students and admirers would be inclined to view any of his truths as arbitrary, Barthes's indictment and stereotypic picture of such thinking in general accurately reflects, I believe, a view common in our time. "Bourgeois ideology," says Barthes (and for bourgeois ideology we may easily read, "Johnsonian common sense") "continuously transforms the products of history into essential types. Just as the cuttlefish squirts its ink in order to protect itself, it cannot rest until it has obscured the ceaseless making of the world, fixated the world into an object which can be forever possessed, catalogued its riches, embalmed it, and injected into reality some purifying essence which will stop its transformation, its flight towards other forms of existence. . . . For the very end of myths is to immobilize the world: they must suggest and mimic a universal order."[5]

For much of our century, Johnson's most habitual modes of thought and most fundamental philosophical assumptions have surely seemed a denial of the flux, multiplicity, and uniqueness of human experience, of the validity of the highly personal vision, of the possibility of personal (or relative) morality. His views must have seemed to many to be historically important and powerfully expressed but not views we can share easily. Modern high school students—and/or their teachers—have been more attracted to fictional heroes who have achieved a highly personal relationship with the culture or the cosmos, who have achieved psychic equilibrium or inner peace outside the system by pursuing "singularity," not by avoiding it. They have read *One Flew Over the Cuckoo's Nest*, not, certainly, *Rasselas* or the *Rambler*. They have been more ready to be moved by the spectacle of the conscious mind coming apart than by the drama of reason and will controlling powerful psychic forces. The idea of literary, historical, and moral absolutes has for a long time seemed an idea whose time has gone, not come. And yet, in spite of all the apparent wisdom implied by this litany of apparent truism, it seems clear to me that the general climate of opinion and sentiment is beginning to change. Not only in the minds of potential young readers, but in the culture itself, there is, I believe, a gradual movement in Johnson's direction once again.

I do not mean to play the role of Partridge and predict impending cultural cataclysm that will wrench us back to the eighteenth century and cause us uncritically to embrace its visions and assumptions. I refer rather to the succession of "other" voices and sentiments one has begun to hear. The makers, shapers, and reflectors of common opinion are in fact beginning to cease to celebrate uncritically our freedom from the supposed restraints and constrictions of common wisdom and shared values. They have begun to reflect more often upon what has been lost or dismissed too hastily in the process of liberation. They have begun to praise consensus and common, rather than personal, values; analytic, rather than visionary, intellectual powers. Here, for example, is one such voice, from a recent *New York Times* book review. The reviewer is Martin Duberman; the book, Robert Fitzgerald's *Enlarging the Change*, an account of the Princeton seminars in literary criticism 1949–51. At the heart of the review is a sense of nostalgia for a consensus about basic critical values, since lost (a pale consensus indeed, in comparison with the one Johnson worked within). The book shows us "how much more confidence existed in nineteen fifty than today about the possibility of literary absolutes. . . . However stifling or narrow or arrogant that community was," Duberman says, "the current anomie attendant on the loss of community is, by contrast, even more debilitating."[6] Strange voices in unlikely places? John Updike strikes a similar note in a different context in a recent *New Yorker* review of *Voices from the Moon*, a novel by Andre Dubus. In particular, the operations and lingering influences of Catholicism upon Dubus's characters capture Updike's imagination. They remind us, he says, "what people used to read novels for. How rare it is, these days, to encounter characters with wills, with a sense of choice. For Jack Kerouac," Updike continues, "Roman Catholicism has dwindled to a manic spark, a frenetic mission to find the sacred everywhere; for Mr. Dubus, amid the self-seeking tangle of secular America, the Church still functions as a standard of measure, a repository of mysteries that can give scale and stature to our lives."[7]

These are not voices crying in the wilderness; they are only two of many. Both reviewers are openly attracted to the ideas of structure, scale derived from standards commonly shared and external to both texts and men; to the ideas of moral choice, a sense of critical community, and greater consensus about the value of moral and aesthetic absolutes. Both writers express what I believe is a growing and far more general dissatisfaction, a sense of needs not being met by the joys of flux and change. They reflect the perceived existence of cultural and psychic vacuums into which nothing in particular seems ready to rush and which, unfortunately, Nature seems not to abhor. They reflect dissatisfaction with current modes of inquiry, conceptual frameworks for conferring meaning and dignity upon texts, individuals, and human relations. And thus, though I see no evidence of resurgence of either neo-Augustanism or neoclassicism, I believe that even college freshmen (taken as the modern embodiment of the famed common reader) are becoming far readier than they have been to appreciate and value intelligently what his vision and values did for a man like Johnson as an artist, writer, critic, and moral agent. Though perhaps we cannot share them, we are becoming less and less able to dismiss all of Johnson's assumptions as arbitrary impositions or as limitations upon our imaginations and critical sensibilities—as blind spots that we end up in one way or another damning by faint praise. I believe students are getting readier not only to read Johnson at all, but to think about what he has to say, and to take his mode of apprehending the world seriously. And I believe that the *Lives* may have some very direct and immediate appeal to modern students, depending on the way we choose to use and teach it.

"Few educated persons," said Eliot, "have read more than half a dozen of [the *Lives*] and of those half dozen, what is remembered is chiefly the passages with which one disagrees."[8] Few educated readers can genuinely be faulted for not having read the lives of Stepney, Pomfret, Tickell, Fenton, and Broome. But the latter portion of Eliot's assertion seems valid and worth considering, for I believe it reflects the way the *Lives* is commonly anthologized and taught. With the notable exception of the Brady and Wimsatt edition of Johnson's selected poetry and prose,[9] virtually all modern collections of Johnson's prose provide only excerpts from the *Lives*, and almost all the excerpts are from the critical rather than the biographical sections. In terms of what is excerpted, there is what amounts to a canon: Johnson on the metaphysical poets (from the *Life of Cowley*); Johnson's famous attack upon *Lycidas;* perhaps some of the better-known salvos directed at Swift; the *Life of Savage* for its power and autobiographical significance; and usually a substantial piece from either *Dryden* or *Pope,* or both, almost always including the famous comparisons: "Dryden's page is a natural field, rising into inequalities and diversified by the varied exuberance of the vegetation; Pope's is a velvet lawn, shaven by the scythe and levelled by the roller" (2:222).

It is a sensible approach, but inevitably it strongly emphasizes the historical importance of Johnson's work. By focusing
on Johnson's most famous pronouncements about *Lycidas* and
the metaphysicals, we end up paying most of our attention to
what we present as more or less magnificent blind spots—like
Johnson's approval of Tate's alterations of *King Lear*. Such
examples are significant because they are either points at
which we feel we must concede our Homer nods, or points at
which the larger aesthetic principles and assumptions reveal
themselves to be limited or inadequate. We talk about Johnson
as a biographer in a tradition; or we emphasize the power of
his prose essentially out of context, or we admire his candor
and balanced view. Though I make no claims beyond my own
experience, I have real doubts about how much such a presentation of Johnson means or can mean to modern students who
have read few, if any, of the works Johnson assesses and who
have little or no command of the critical and conceptual contexts needed to appreciate his achievement fully. Such an
approach certainly hurts no one, but I am not persuaded that it
genuinely exploits the *Lives'* potential appeal.

As a classroom teacher, I have encountered similar problems with the many current scholarly approaches to the *Lives*.
On the one hand, I think it is fair to say that much of the best
and most rewarding critical work done with the *Lives* or with
Johnson's literary criticism (drawing heavily upon the *Lives*)
has been done in the past several decades. Professor Folkenflik's comprehensive study of the *Lives* as biography[10]
comes to mind immediately, as does the string of impressive
studies of Johnson's criticism, beginning with that of Jean
Hagstrum and including more recent books like those by
Leopold Damrosch and William Edinger.[11] On the other hand,
though books written at these levels of sophistication provide
vital background for working scholars and teachers of more or
less advanced courses, their most sophisticated and intriguing
points often need considerable mediation before they will
make any sense to or have any impact upon freshmen and
sophomores in introductory courses. When I depend at all

heavily upon such material in beginning courses, I find that I end up talking as much about the history and nature of biography as about the texts themselves. Or I find myself talking about aesthetic theory to confused (though interested) sophomores who take copious notes but haven't the faintest idea what the notes mean. And yet, naive or foolish as it may sound to some, I genuinely believe it is time to begin to include Johnson more regularly in introductory courses—in both high school and college. I would like, therefore, to suggest a somewhat different approach.

I think, in part, that "tense" is the answer. I think we have to emphasize what Johnson *does*—not what he *did*. To that end, my first suggestion is the undramatic and perhaps obvious one that it is better to teach one or two lives whole than snippets from four or five. Teaching the complete text allows students to *see* the work whole and observe Johnson performing the continuous critical act of assessing both life and works. It allows them to follow both sustained analysis and fully developed train of thought. The lives most often excerpted and included in anthologies—Cowley, Milton, Swift, Pope, and Savage—make the most sense. (The *Life of Savage* is frequently printed entire and the Brady and Wimsatt edition offers a fine selection of whole lives.) Read whole, the lives provide a sustained look at Johnson's mind at work upon a subject worthy of its powers. And rather than attempting to arouse student interest primarily by arguments from literary history or critical blind spots, I suggest emphasizing instead what I believe to be the inherent interest in Johnson's habitual modes of inquiry and assessment, specifically his methods of analysis and his extraordinary ability to generalize.

Walter Jackson Bate observes that "the common statement about Johnson's literary criticism is that even when Johnson is plainly in the wrong, he incites more thought than critics who are or seem to be in the right."[12] Johnson's particular mode of analytic generalization is surely one of the reasons this may be so.

One of Johnson's most underrated and frequently misperceived powers is his ability to generalize; and the better-known lives provide abundant, extended examples of his ability, not to utter canned wisdom in a particularly forceful way, but to examine, explore, assess, and make sense of the data of human experience. That generalizing is completely different from simply being general (as in freshman essays) is a distinction lost, I believe, on a substantial number of our students. If my experience is at all typical, few have even had much practice summarizing. And yet, in the context of renewed emphasis on the ability to think critically and analytically—to "process information" and "problem solve" (to use the current buzz words)—I think students may be ready to view Johnson in a decidedly new light. The Johnson of traditional stereotype suffered from the imputation of pomposity and pontification. His heavily Latinate diction was often made fun of in his own day when, as Goldsmith observed, "he made the little fishes talk like whales." And of course, by selective quotation, one can still trivialize him in this way. But in fact, nothing is farther from pomposity, shallow moralizing, or conventional wisdom than the relentless and subtle analytic powers of Johnson's mind, his command of language and control of concentric contexts of meaning. It is one thing, that is, smugly to utter phrases like "all that glitters is not gold" or "sin in haste, repent at leisure," and quite another to make generalization a process of seeking and enlarging meaning rather than simply applying or imposing it. The following from the *Life of Swift* is a good example. "It may be justly supposed," Johnson says,

> that there was in [Swift's] conversation, what appears so frequently in his letters, an affectation of familiarity with the great, an ambition of momentary equality sought and enjoyed by the neglect of those ceremonies which custom has established as the barriers between one order of society and another. This transgression of regularity was by himself and his admirers termed greatness of soul. But a great mind disdains to hold anything by courtesy, and therefore never usurps what a lawful claimant may take away. He that encroaches on another's dignity puts him-

self in his power: he is either repelled with helpless in-
dignity, or endured by clemency and condescension.
[3:61]

The passage is an absolutely typical example of Johnson's
method in the biographical portions of the *Lives*. The initial
generalization places Swift's behavior in the larger category of
all those who affect familiarity with the great. It is followed by
a clause that further explains the dynamics and the implications of the act ("by the neglect of those ceremonies which
custom has established . . ."). Johnson then supplies a still
larger context in which to view the subject and introduces
another standard against which to judge it: If Swift and his
friends thought such behavior greatness of soul, the "great
mind disdains to hold anything by courtesy." This is no simple
application of a common truth. What Johnson means is that
the mind *ought* to disdain to hold anything by courtesy. It is by
no means what oft is thought but simply ne'er so well expressed. It is precisely *not* what might have sprung instantly to
the average reader's mind, and it makes us think about the
subject in a more complex way, by enlarging the context of our
awareness. Then comes the final generalization that stamps
the passage as quintessentially Johnsonian: "He that en-
croaches on another's dignity puts himself in his power."
Though it is possible to view this assertion as a sort of "nug-
get"—the lesson to be remembered and repeated—I believe it
is something quite different. What does it mean to say that we
put ourselves in another's power by becoming overfamiliar?
Johnson's concluding clauses ("he is either repelled . . . or
endured . . .") explain, but only in general terms. I think it is
worth asking students to provide concrete answers and examples from their own lives—to test the idea by the challenge of
applying it, because all generalization does not invite intellectual closure or imply finality. Johnson's generalizations constantly channel or refract ideas outward; they provoke
thought, because they invite personal application. They are
not a signal that discussion has ended (as some of his famous

conversational jewels clearly are); they are an invitation to reflection.

It may be legitimate to argue that formulaic folk wisdom, maxims (even those as subtle as La Rochefoucauld's), and certain kinds of aphoristic thought either have a circular or tautological quality about them, or that they pigeonhole and simplify the complexities of human experience. But not Johnson's. Certainly most scholars and close readers of Johnson's own writings have been aware of this distinction all along. But, for the common reader, Johnson's reputation has clearly suffered from the fact that it is his wonderful conversational wit that is easiest to remember, that springs first to people's minds, and that characterizes his intellectual abilities best. How hard it would be to repeat an extended passage like the above, and how simple and attractive (by comparison) to repeat lines like "Patriotism is the last refuge of a scoundrel," or "A woman's preaching is like a dog's walking upon its hind legs. . . ." Yet these and the like are not typical examples of Johnson's analytic powers or his strength as a critic, biographer, or moral writer. His strength is his mode of inquiry itself. Though the structure of his sentences may imply intellectual closure, and the famed balances and antitheses reflect control and symmetry, the trains of thought started and pursued and the ideas implied often extend well beyond the structures that contain them. Almost any subject can set the full intellectual process in motion. A good example is Johnson's reflections on the apparently trivial subject of Pope's grotto. "A grotto," Johnson observes, "is not often the wish or pleasure of an Englishman, who has more frequent need to solicit than exclude the sun." Johnson then begins to pursue the thought, by providing possible answers to the implied question he has raised: Why would Pope have built a grotto? The first possibility: "Pope's excavation was requisite as an entrance to his garden, and, as some men try to be proud of their defects, he extracted an ornament from an inconvenience." This suggestion is followed by a series of speculations generated by the possible implications of the first. "It may be frequently remarked of the studious and speculative," Johnson continues, "that they are proud of trifles, and that their amusements seem frivolous and childish; whether it be that men conscious of great reputation think themselves above the reach of censure, and safe in the admission of negligent indulgences, or that mankind expect from the elevated genius an uniformity of greatness, and watch its degradation with malicious wonder" (3:135). This sequence of ideas is what I would call exploratory generalization. It does not sum up or preclude further thought; it expands the ideas and pursues a train of thought outward toward possibilities. It is not a more or less mechanical application of a convenient universal truth; it is the visible and outward sign of a sophisticated mode of rational inquiry that involves command of language and concepts, the application of acquired knowledge and personal experience, and the constant evaluation of the data of human experience. The passage ends with a simile, not a maxim. Such watchers and judgers of the great may be, Johnson concludes, "like him who having followed with his eyes an eagle into the clouds should lament that she ever descended to a perch." Not a platitude, but a complex, thought-provoking image. I think all one need do to help students appreciate the mental acts required for such sustained generalization is require them to try to perform them themselves, compare the results with Johnson's, and then discuss the differences.

I believe that Johnson's literary criticism can be made more accessible as well and also without recourse primarily to arguments for historical importance or discussion of blind spots. Yet again, the task may seem formidable for all the reasons mentioned above. An almost random look at the textual criticism in the *Life of Cowley*, for instance, provides examples of critical standards based on assumptions few modern readers share, applied to texts few modern students have ever read. "The great pleasure of verse arises from the known measure of the lines and uniform structure of the stanzas, by which the voice is regulated and the memory relieved" (1:47; observed in a discussion of Cowley's Pindaric odes); "Truth is always truth, and reason is always reason" (1:59; from a general discussion of Cowley's diction).

Not very promising material, one might say. Both quotes exemplify an utterly typical Johnsonian critical act: the statement of a general standard in the context of which a particular text or some aspect of it is judged. Sometimes the standards Johnson applies still make perfect sense at first reading and, thus, pose no problems for modern readers ("imitations produce pain or pleasure not because they are mistaken for realities, but because they bring realities to mind," the dismissal of the unities problems in Shakespeare, and so on). Sometimes it is not so easy to accept Johnson's standards ("Vice . . . should always disgust. . . . Whenever it appears it should raise hatred.") And sometimes—often, in fact—it becomes clear that Johnson's standards and assumptions deserve careful thought, both to understand their implications fully and to decide how viable they yet may be. Students often do not need to know the particular texts in question to respond to the standards and assumptions Johnson uses and the mode of inquiry he employs. And they do not necessarily need to approach Johnson's aesthetic criteria as historical curiosities; there is no reason why they should not take them on their own terms and think about them. I would encourage them to do so, because all critics and virtually anyone performing a conscious critical act proceeds on the basis of assumptions about things like how our minds work when we write and read, how words and language "mean," the roles fiction and poetry perform for us. The most basic assumptions usually go entirely unexamined. We don't question their existence any more than we question (or doubt) the existence of telephones or electricity. They are part of our daily mental lives, and because they seem so obvious we seldom see them. It is useful, I believe, to bring such assumptions to consciousness once in a while, to look at them critically and perhaps challenge them.

No matter how many opportunities students have to learn, the majority develop fairly late a sense of aesthetic theory and of the larger questions literature and language invite, if they develop it at all. Often they have a few nameable, categorizable methods to apply to texts and these methods usually represent the sum of the influences of their best (or worst) teachers. A few

may even have a sense of historical perspective to the extent
that they are aware, for example, that at other times people
applied different criteria for judging. Yet what frequently un-
derlies such notions is a surprisingly close analogue of the
eighteenth century's myth of progress: the idea that modern
ideas—building upon the presumed mistakes of the past—are
of necessity more advanced and therefore better (rather than
simply different). Where art and not technology is concerned,
this is neither a proven fact nor a particularly useful attitude.
Criticism, in any age, is not a science. It is a mode of inquiry.
And it is always appropriate to remind our students and ourselves that, as Professor Abrams puts it, "Because many critical statements of fact are . . . partially relative to the perspective of the theory within which they occur, they are not
'true' in the strict scientific sense that they approach the ideal
of being verifiable by any human being, no matter what his
point of view."[13] What with the New Critic's positions now
being explained in footnotes, it is well to remind ourselves that
such as Chaucer is shall Derrida be. It is extremely healthy, I
think, to encourage a greater sense of catholicity and critical
relativism in our students, a sense that Johnson's critical vision is more than just a particular historical moment in a
linear progression. Rather, his criticism is an example of a way
of approaching and judging literary texts that we can disagree
with and yet learn much from.

A close look at Johnson's anlyses of particular texts in any of
the major lives can provide an ideal opportunity to raise the
sort of critical issues and questions that students might profit
from by confronting early rather than late. For example, when
Johnson praises the song of Comus by suggesting, "the invita-
tions to pleasure are so general that they excite no distinct
images of corrupt enjoyment and take no dangerous hold on
the fancy," he is making quite definite assumptions about how
our minds work when we read a literary text. Forget the fact
that students may not have read *Comus;* the logic and implications of the statement can be discussed on their own terms.
What assumptions does Johnson make when he asserts that
general images of corruption take no dangerous hold on the

fancy? I don't think it is a bad tactic to ask students to para-
phrase such a statement, put it into modern language, and
discuss it if there is disagreement about meanings. How do
modern students imagine that *their* minds work when they
read a literary text? My experience suggests that few have
thought about it. When students are pressed for their own
explanations, how do their answers differ from Johnson's?
What does either view of the mind suggest about the powers
and responsibilities of the writer? Johnson's critical portions
of the *Lives* are rife with examples of his critical thinking so
that this sort of branching series of questions can be started by
any of the *Lives* and almost any page in the sections devoted to
textual analyses. For instance, Johnson observes in the *Life of
Dryden* that, until Dryden, there was "no poetical diction, no
system of words at once refined from the grossness of domestic
use, and free from the harshness of terms appropriated to
particular arts. Words too familiar, or too remote, defeat the
purpose of a poet. From those sounds which we hear on small
or coarse occasions, we do not easily receive strong impressions, or delightful images" (1:420).

Is this true? (Is it not?) Many modern students are initially
put off by the abstract diction and what seems the otherwise
stilted, formal, and artificial language of eighteenth-century
poetry, because whether they know it or not they have fairly
definite assumptions about things like the kind of language
and subjects appropriate for poetry, the social role of poetry,
and the pleasure for the reader. What are those assumptions?
How adequately can they defend them? How often do students
examine them or even bring them fully to consciousness? I
believe that students are more accustomed to hearing or reading summary generalizations about such matters than to
doing some of the spadework themselves. The *Lives* provides
chance after chance for them to do so. Where the process of
inquiry goes is, in a sense, irrelevant; it is the act of questioning itself that seems to me most likely to teach students about
both Johnson's thinking and their own. "Within his range,"
says Eliot, "within his time, Johnson had as fine an ear as
anybody. Again and again, when he calls attention to beauties

or to blemishes in the work of the poets of whom he writes, we must acknowledge . . . that he is pointing out something we might not have noticed independently. It may prove that his criteria are permanently relevant."[14] It may prove so; it may not. The value for students is in the close examination of his premises and assumptions and the subsequent clarification of their own.

In sum, I believe that modern students are likely to be increasingly willing to give Johnson a hearing, and for reasons that have, it seems to me, a surprisingly familiar ring. At the risk of appearing to embrace neoclassical views naively or uncritically, we find it increasingly hard not to have a more or less classical sense of history as endless cycles, rather than linear progression. For instance, we are being told again—by particle physicists, not Bishop Berkeley—that the solidity of objects is really an illusion. The specter of mechanism that so troubled Boswell has returned in yet another form. For though B.F. Skinner has been more or less defanged (or defrocked?) the psychobiologists are now telling us that our limbic systems may do more than Milton can to justify our ways to Man. We are told we no longer have a permanent Self, which we can discover and be true to. We create and recreate ourselves— almost daily—by playing roles. There is no "us," only "we." "The world of experience," the cognitive scientists tell us, "is produced by the man who experiences it"[15] (shades of both Hume and Berkeley). And so on, in context after context. And these are not theories debated only by philosophers. In simplified forms, they have all become or are becoming more or less a part of the common view of things. Could there be a better time for modern students, intellectually afloat on a vast and shifting sea, to see Johnson not as cumbersome intellectual baggage but as genuinely attractive ballast? Not as a millstone, but as an anchor?

There is a current theory that the world—the realities we see when we look around us—is perceived quite differently by different animal species. "The real world we know intuitively," says Dr. Harry Jerison, "is a creation of the nervous system, a model of a possible world which enables the nervous system to handle the enormous amount of information it receives and processes. . . . *The work of the brain is to create the model of a possible world rather than record or transmit a world that is metaphysically true"* (my emphasis).[16] This is only a theory at present and it is obviously a position with which Johnson himself would have disagreed, perhaps violently. But it raises some interesting philosophical questions that are potentially relevant here. For we do not need to endorse the idea completely to hypothesize that as with different species, so with successive generations of critics and philosophers; each proceeds to judge texts and/or human beings—to explain literary effects and human behavior—on the basis of a model of a possible world that enables the critics to handle the enormous amount of information they receive and process rather than to record or transmit a view that is metaphysically true. Perhaps, in fact, Pope is right and, with generations of critics at least, "'tis with our judgements as our watches, none go just alike, yet each believes his own." Eliot suggests that "it remains to be seen whether the literary influence of Johnson . . . does not merely await a generation which has not yet been born to receive it."[17] I believe that generation is nearer at hand than we suspect. And if I am right, it will most likely be for the qualities of Johnson's mind, qualities that simply transcend any problems modern students may have with language that at first seems difficult and archaic and with assumptions about the role of literature they do not share, that this generation will receive Johnson's influence. It will be for reasons that are abundantly clear in the *Lives of the Poets* and that Boswell very precisely identified over two centuries ago. "Johnson's superiority over other learned men consisted chiefly in what may be called the art of thinking, the art of using his mind; a certain continual power of seizing the useful substance of all that he knew, and exhibiting it in a clear and forcible manner; so that knowledge, which we often see to be no better than lumber in men of dull understanding, was, in him, true, evident, and actual wisdom."[18]

Boswell is seldom given credit for his ability to analyze Johnsonian complexity; but his estimate of these particular

Johnsonian abilities can scarcely be improved on. Johnson's wisdom is of a kind that is not static knowledge; it is not a fixed sum of stored learning and experience to be drawn upon as if it were in a bank. It is a way of knowing, a means of questioning experience and pursuing truth. When we invite students to study Johnson, we are not asking them to study what he thought; we are inviting them to learn about thinking.

MICHAEL STUPRICH

Johnson and Biography: Recent Critical Directions

Coming to grips in a few pages with the past fifteen years of Johnson studies can seem a little too much like wrestling Antaeus: balancing the opponent overhead can quickly prove to be a tiring proposition, but going to ground with him is likely only to produce new complications. Perhaps the major difficulty, not surprisingly, is the abundance of available materials; as the MLA's annual bibliography continues along the road to corpulence, letting out its belt several notches each year, the section devoted to Johnson swells happily along with it, perhaps putting cynics in mind of Johnson's trenchant remarks concerning "the epidemical conspiracy for the destruction of paper." And yet even a cursory search through the listings will remind us that the period since 1970 has been a particularly rich one in terms of quality as well. Through 1978 alone, for example, we were presented with a number of important books, including perhaps the finest study of Johnson's criticism since the work of Hagstrum and Keast, and several important lives of Johnson, one of which, arguably the modern standard for Johnson biography, added new fuel to the ongoing controversy over the aims and methods of Johnson scholarship in general.

Luckily, the focus of this collection—Johnson and biography—provides a limiting principle. And yet once we recall Johnson's belief that no other kind of writing "can be more delightful or more useful" than biography, and once we begin cataloguing those of his works that in some way employ biography, a new complication looms, that of selection. Given the high moral purpose that Johnson characteristically assigned to literature in general and to biography in particular, it is not surprising to find his biographical theories and practices figuring more or less prominently in all the book-length studies, though only one, Robert Folkenflik's impressive *Samuel Johnson, Biographer*, deals exclusively with the subject. In these cases, selection can be based only on the amount of space given over to our topic. Thus Leopold Damrosch's *The Uses of Johnson's Criticism*, a major contribution to the canon, is included, while his earlier but in many ways equally interesting *Samuel Johnson and the Tragic Sense* (Princeton, 1972) is not. When faced with the several hundred shorter works that deserve consideration, the bibliographer's problem of selection grows more acute. If we include only those works that deal with Johnson's "straight" biographies, from the very early *Life of Sarpi* through the *Lives of the Poets*, what do we do with those dealing with, say, *The Vanity of Human Wishes*, with its long procession of biographical vignettes, or with *Rasselas*, which, whatever else we might decide to label it, is at one level at least a fictionalized biography?

The extent to which these problems can be solved will be indicated by the bibliography which follows these prefatory remarks. This listing is intended as an aid to further research, and as such can be taken as a partial supplement to Clifford and Greene's indispensable *Samuel Johnson: A Survey and Bibliography of Critical Studies* (Minneapolis, 1970), still far and away the most comprehensive guide to pre-1970 works. Any number of significant works are here made conspicuous by their absence, including the biographies alluded to above, all of which have useful things to say about Johnson as biographer but are generally well known and easily accessible. The listed works are essentially of two kinds: studies of Johnson's sources for various of the lives, and critical evaluations of Johnson's biographical theories and/or practices, both in general and in the more specific contexts provided by examinations of individual lives. In some cases, as in Folkenflik's study, both concerns are rewardingly engaged through a syncretic approach. The following brief survey reviews works that seem particularly significant or useful, referred to here by author's name and title; full citations appear in the bibliography.

Of the dozen or so notable works produced by Johnson during the first years of his association with Edward Cave and the *Gentleman's Magazine*, many are biographies; and even in his first published work, the translation of Father Lobo's *Voyage to Abyssinia* (1735), we can clearly detect his growing fascination with the kind of solid, "verifiable" truth he believed that biography alone could provide. The six-year period, then, from the *Life of Sarpi* (1738) through his first major—and first "literary"—biography, the *Life of Savage* (1744), is obviously of importance to anyone interested in Johnson's development as a biographer. Unfortunately, except for the scattered commentary offered by Folkenflik, we have only one recent treatment of this period and its problems, John J. Burke's cogent and informative essay, "Excellence in Biography: *Rambler* No. 60 and Johnson's Early Biographies." Burke's design here is to rescue these works from critical obscurity by viewing them as early embodiments of the biographical theories Johnson formulated several years later in the famous *Rambler* essay, which Burke sees as a "criticism and vindication" of Johnson's initial practices as a biographer. Until the situation is remedied by the Yale editors, serious work with these early biographies will be hampered by the lack of accessible, authoritative texts.[1] In *Early Biographical Writings of Dr. Johnson*, J.D. Fleeman has provided facsimile reprints of all these rarely collected lives, although the printing technique has rendered several of them virtually unreadable. Fleeman's introduction, though brief, contains a helpful catalogue of dates and facts.

If critics have had little to say about these early lives, they have had a very great deal indeed to say about the *Life of Savage*, making it, at least in terms of critical interest, the most popular of all Johnson's biographies. For a number of reasons, of course, *Savage* occupies a unique position in the canon of Johnsonian biography. There is, for one thing, its chronological importance: written in 1744, it rests precisely midway between *Sarpi* and *Rambler* 60, and thus provides a nice opportunity for studying both Johnson's developing technical skills as a biographer and his increasing awareness of the moral and didactic potentialities of biography as a literary art. *Savage* is also notable as Johnson's first sally into the field of literary biography, his first attempt to explore the connections between the artist and the man. Thus, by pointing forward not only to *Rambler* 60 but more importantly to the *Lives of the Poets*, *Savage* becomes a crucial document, the first major step in a process that culminates grandly in those two masterpieces of literary biography, the lives of Dryden and Pope.

But the chief reason for the continuing interest in *Savage* probably lies elsewhere—in the intriguingly personal and complex relationship between Johnson and Savage. For in *Savage*, as in no other of Johnson's biographical works, we can see the biographer interacting personally with his subject, reporting not just what he has gathered secondhand from others, but what he has seen and heard himself, and then using the physical data as the basis for psychological inference. Johnson's search throughout is for the keys to Savage's behavior, and the classic ethical premise he works from holds that we can only know a man by his actions. To understand Savage, then, we as readers must come to understand why he acts as he does. To this end Johnson constantly places himself between his reader and his material, working to control and modify our responses to each incident, each succeeding act in the drama of Savage's life. And the *Life of Savage* can be seen as successful, it seems, precisely to the degree that Johnson's often quirky mediation is either accepted as a given or considered as aesthetically necessary. Earlier quibbles about the technique of *Savage*—such as Joseph Wood Krutch's testiness over Johnson's "preposterous partiality"[2]—have recently given way to more sympathetic treatments, which generally begin by recognizing the many difficulties Johnson faced when

he sat down in 1744 to compose this "mournful narrative" of
his friend's life.

Among recent studies of *Savage*, perhaps the most satisfying
is William Vesterman's account of "Johnson and *The Life of
Savage*." A work as rich as *Savage* of course allows for any
number of critical approaches, but Vesterman seems correct in
focusing on Johnson's role as mediator and on his consequent
search for the "proper judges" of Savage's conduct—a search
that naturally ends with Johnson himself, whose own proper
judgments are complexly embodied in what Vesterman terms
his "greater style." This style, in part arising from and governed by a pattern of legal metaphors that subtly reinforce
Johnson's part as mediator-judge, allows him to avoid "the
melodramatic reactions his material almost irresistibly
urges" and moreover to transform the particular incidents of
Savage's life into something more permanent and more useful,
something like those "parallel circumstances and kindred images" that can offer "instruction to every diversity of condition."[3]

Even under Johnson's magisterial guidance, however, coming to understand Savage's misanthropy can be a difficult task.
How can we respond with the necessary sympathy, for instance, to the many episodes in which Savage displays his
outrageous pride? To, say, his refusing a desperately needed
suit of clothes because it was offered "with some neglect of
courtesy"? As Vesterman suggests, a completely sympathetic
response to such behavior is sometimes too much to ask—of
Johnson, of ourselves. Something of a dilemma results: Johnson's moral honesty will not allow him to exclude such hard
facts, and his style, though generous in the judgments it en-
forces, cannot adequately temper them. Johnson's only recourse, then, is to irony, a complicated gesture whereby he
momentarily retreats a few steps from the events at hand and
aligns himself with us, against Savage.

Martin Maner, in an essay on "Satire and Sympathy in
Johnson's *Life of Savage*," also detects these moments of emerging irony, but finds them commensurate with Johnson's narrative technique, which "uses emotional conflict as a way of

shaping the reader's attitude toward Savage." Rejecting as too narrow Vesterman's conception of Johnson's "style," Maner offers instead a pattern of authorial intercession through which Johnson "arouses expectations of emotional release, then frustrates these expectations by bringing other emotions into play." Maner sees this pattern as effective across the entire spectrum of reader response, ranging from "complete sympathetic identification" with Savage at one end, to "complete detachment" at the other. Savage, however, for all his follies and posturings, is hardly an appropriate target for satiric ridicule: he has suffered too much, at too many people's hands, and Johnson, who has himself witnessed examples of that suffering, is not about to indulge in easy laughter at his friend's expense. Instead, as Maner acutely points out, Johnson is always ready to shift his satiric focus to more deserving targets—the notorious Countess Macclesfield among others—and to employ Savage as a satiric spokesman against them, thus perhaps allowing Savage in death what had always eluded him in life, the last laugh.

Readers of *Savage* have long been puzzled by the extent of Johnson's hostility toward the countess; indeed, he seems to regard her with a kind of melodramatic horror, as a creature not altogether human in her capacity for cold and motiveless evil. In John Dussinger's interesting account of "Style and Intention in Johnson's *Life of Savage*," the countess is seen as one of several treacherous, "Circean" females who conspire to defeat Savage at every turn, and Johnson's overt hostility is primarily explained by his fear of any force destructive of the family and the "conservative, patriarchal social order," which has the family as its foundation and "subordination" as its operative principle. Though sometimes a bit top-heavy in its Freudianism, Dussinger's essay is elegantly written and generally persuasive.

Of the several book-length studies that include discussions of *Savage*, two are especially interesting: Folkenflik's *Samuel Johnson, Biographer* and Damrosch's *The Uses of Johnson's Criticism*. Folkenflik's decision to devote a full chapter to *Savage* is disappointing only in what it excludes. Given the sanity

of his opinions and the scope of his research, one would naturally like to see more extended work on the *Lives of the Poets*.
Still, his discussion of Savage as a "tragic hero *manqué*" is a
valuable contribution. Though he devotes only a few pages to
Savage, Damrosch nevertheless manages to provide a welcome
tonic effect in his "perhaps heretical notion" that Johnson "is
not at his best" in *Savage* though what he gives us is "a brilliant
work . . . expressed in a style in which irony is perfectly balanced with sympathy."

Finally, Frank Ellis's article on "Johnson and Savage: Two
Failed Tragedies and a Failed Tragic Hero" deserves mention
for its novel discussion of *Savage* in terms of two plays, one
totally forgotten and the other preserved only because of its
author's later accomplishments: Savage's *The Tragedy of Sir
Thomas Overbury* and Johnson's *Irene*.

Johnson did not equal the biographical excellence of *Savage*
for another thirty-five years, though in this long interim period
during which he grew from an anonymous Grub Street hack
into England's foremost man of letters he produced a number
of biographies. Coming to these, one is immediately struck not
so much by their quality—though competent they are hardly
inspired—as by their range; whether his subject is Edward
Cave or Frederick the Great, Johnson seems equally comfortable, proving by example his belief that "there has rarely
passed a life of which a judicious and faithful narrative would
not be useful." By itself, however, this body of material is not
substantial enough to support extensive critical inquiry. We
have in fact only one recent study of a biography from this
period, James Lill's "A Lesson in Futurity: Johnson's *Life of Sir
Thomas Browne*." Though long cited as a major influence on
Johnson, Browne presented several problems to his biographer; his buoyant religious optimism and his irritating cir-
cumlocutions, for instance, must have carried Johnson's patience to its limits. And yet, as Lill writes, Johnson grows to
admire his subject in spite of these problems, gradually sur-
rendering to "Browne's spell" and coming to find in the "totality" of his life "both useful knowledge and exemplary
conviction." Additional commentary on *Browne* and the re-

mainder of the biographical works between *Savage* and the *Lives of the Poets* can be found in Folkenflik; reprints of all but one of these lives (the prefatory biography of Zachary Pierce) are included in Fleeman's collection. A valuable perspective on Johnson's critical positions during these years is given by Mark Kinkead-Weekes in his essay discussing "Johnson on 'The Rise of the Novel.' " In his attempt to explain Johnson's notoriously disproportionate praise of Richardson at Fielding's expense, Kinkead-Weekes points to an important change in Johnson's thinking: the increasing "sense of complexity in character and consciousness" produced by his "immersion in Shakespeare." Kinkead-Weekes's ideas are especially interesting when set alongside Damrosch's contention that the *Preface to Shakespeare* "is transitional rather than central in [Johnson's] critical writing, a work that poses problems which will be solved much more successfully in the *Lives of the Poets.*"

Praised by Boswell as "the richest, most beautiful, and indeed most perfect, production of Johnson's pen," the *Lives of the Poets* seems today a fitting capstone to Johnson's long career. For in this work, which began modestly enough as "little Lives, with little Prefaces," we can see Johnson working toward a grand summation, not only of a literary tradition he clearly cherished, but of his own life and views as well. By allowing himself to be "led beyond my intention . . . by the honest desire of giving useful pleasure," Johnson gives much more. Defining and evaluating this "more" is exactly the task a critic undertakes when he comes to the *Lives*. Luckily, although we have relatively few studies that survey the *Lives* as a whole, the few we have are excellent.

William McCarthy's "The Moral Art of Johnson's *Lives*" and Mark W. Booth's "Proportion and Value in Johnson's *Lives of the Poets*" offer ideally complementary introductions to this work whose scope and variety make it particularly intimidating. Concise and informed, both essays provide a number of rewarding insights. McCarthy, for example, wisely reminds modern readers that Johnson's "idea of how to write a life differs from ours" before proceeding to place Johnson relative to "the English biographical tradition of Cavendish, John Foxe,

Walton, Fuller, Aubrey, and Anthony à Wood." The bulk of McCarthy's essay is given over to an analysis of the "thematic gestures" of Johnson's specific biographical genre—the "brief life." By characterizing the *Lives* as Johnson's "deeply ironic" "survey of the human condition," McCarthy is able to pull together the seemingly disparate threads running through the work into a single unifying theme that recognizes and asserts "that man is by nature a tragic character." This theme, McCarthy suggests, is epitomized in the *Life of Swift*, a virtual "Shakespearian tragedy in the guise of a prose narrative, and . . . a major moral center of the *Lives* as a whole."

Although Booth's notion of how Johnson "proportions" the fifty-two lives is quite helpful, his most valuable contribution is rather his sense of the ultimate purpose behind Johnson's scheme. In Booth's view, "The story told by all the *Lives* is an evaluative history. It is an attempt to assess and understand the cumulative achievement of all those writers. As it elaborates an ordered whole from separate parts, it builds a structure that is Samuel Johnson's understanding of the age in which he has done his own work." Recalling Johnson's distaste for the poetry of his own day ("One bad ode may be suffered; but a number of them together makes one sick"), we might also consider the *Lives* as a kind of elegy, Johnson's last tribute to a poetic tradition that had clearly run its course.

Two more theoretically minded studies are also of interest. Booth's earlier essay on "Johnson's Critical Judgments in the *Lives of the Poets*" examines Johnson's method of apportioning praise and blame in the *Lives* and concludes that "everything in Johnson's criticism here is somehow corrective. Nothing he says is calculated to leave the reader's opinion undisturbed." In his essay discussing "Johnson's Form of Evaluation," Robert DeMaria's purpose is "to illuminate a pattern of language in terms of which Johnson perceives, describes, and evaluates literature." He does so in intriguing ways, suggesting, for example, that the "archetypal form of Johnson's descriptive evaluations" was inherited from Dryden and "rewritten" in various ways to fit the occasions of its use, particularly in the *Lives*.

One other essay deserves mention for its value as an introduction to the *Lives*. This is Pat Rogers's fine source study, "Johnson's *Lives of the Poets* and the Biographic Dictionaries." After identifying "three broad categories" of biographical writings that served Johnson as "sources and models," Rogers considers with great care Johnson's "general working method" in putting together the biographical sections of the *Lives*. Rogers's scholarly investigations have saved a great many students of Johnson a great deal of time.

The two works that examine the *Lives* most rewardingly and most completely are Lawrence Lipking's *The Ordering of the Arts in Eighteenth-Century England* and Damrosch's *The Uses of Johnson's Criticism*. Lipking's work is more historically oriented than Damrosch's, more concerned with placing the *Lives* with those other eighteenth-century works (like Burney's *History of Music*) that "strove to present the whole range of an art." Damrosch, on the other hand, is concerned almost exclusively with the *Lives* as the arena in which Johnson's characteristic "way of thinking about life and literature" achieves its fullest expression. Consequently, Lipking can offer a somewhat more complete picture of the *Lives* as an artistic whole, while Damrosch is able to deal more comprehensively with the nature and development of Johnson's critical opinions and their applications in the *Lives*. Happily, these two works seldom overlap and are almost never at odds with each other; taken together they provide us with what is thus far the finest examination of Johnson's crowning achievement.

Of the fifty-two biographies comprising the *Lives of the Poets*, none has elicited quite the controversy of the *Life of Milton*. The issue is no longer so emotional as when Cowper longed to "thresh" Johnson's jacket "till I made his pension jingle in his pocket," and the contemporary Miltonists have even occasionally acknowledged the justice of some of Johnson's verdicts, but Johnson's seeming antipathy to Milton remains problematic. The classic line of defense for Johnsonians has taken Johnson's personal dislike of Milton as a given and worked from there to argue that Johnson's respect for Milton's work forced him to a rigorous separation of Milton the man from Milton the artist. This is more or less the line taken by both Lipking and Damrosch, though Folkenflik argues that "Johnson perceives a relationship between the character of Milton and his writings" but "is unwilling to see any deterministic relationship between the two." An interesting perspective on this question is provided by Stephen Fix in his fine essay "Distant Genius: Johnson and the Art of Milton's Life." For Fix, "the real achievement, difficulty, and excitement of the *Life of Milton* is precisely that Johnson actively sought to connect Milton's life and art." In so doing, Johnson was searching not for "biographical interpretations of specific poems" but rather for the evidence in "Milton's life and character" that would best "explain his unusual combination of artistic talents and deficiencies." The "distant genius" of Fix's title illuminates the core of Johnson's explanation: Milton's "remoteness from common life," his freedom from the "constraints of the experiential world," was what allowed him finally, in Johnson's words, "to sport in the wide regions of possibility"—to create, that is, a work as rich and as enduring as *Paradise Lost.*

An essay of this sort really requires no conclusion beyond, perhaps, the sincere wish that the next fifteen years of Johnson scholarship might be even more productive than the last. We have yet a great deal to learn from Johnson, and he is nowhere a more eloquent or more effective teacher than in his biographical writings. These "experiences in living," as Walter Jackson Bate calls them, provided Johnson with the ideal vehicles for communicating those stores of wit and moral wisdom accumulated over a long and full life. Thus a collection like the present one, devoted to reexamining and redefining the major issues of Johnsonian biography, can serve to light the way to future work.

Bibliography

This selected bibliography makes no claims of comprehensiveness and is intended to supplement the bibliographic work in James L. Clifford and Donald J. Greene, *Samuel Johnson: A Survey and Bibli-*

ography of Critical Studies (Minneapolis: Univ. of Minnesota Press, 1970) and in the earlier William P. Courtney and D. Nichol Smith, *A Bibliography of Samuel Johnson* (Oxford: Clarendon, 1915, 1925) and Robert William Chapman and Allen T. Hazen, "Johnsonian Bibliography: A Supplement to Courtney," *Proceedings of the Oxford Bibliographical Society* 5 (1939): 119-66.

Abbott, John L. "Samuel Johnson and 'The Life of Dr. Richard Mede.' " *Bulletin of the John Rylands Library* 54 (1971): 12–22.

Alkon, Paul Kent. "The Intention and Reception of Johnson's *Life of Savage.*" *Modern Philology* 72, No. 2 (Nov. 1974): 139–50.

Batten, Charles L., Jr. "Samuel Johnson's Sources for 'The Life of Roscommon.' " *Modern Philology* 72, No. 2 (Nov. 1974): 185–89.

Battersby, James L. "Johnson and Shiels: Biographers of Addison." *Studies in English Literature* 9 (1969): 521–37.

———. *Rational Praise and Natural Lamentation: Johnson, Lycidas, and Principles of Criticism.* Rutherford, N.J.: Fairleigh Dickinson Univ. Press, 1980.

Booth, Mark W. "Johnson's Critical Judgments in the *Lives of the Poets.*" *Studies in English Literature* 16 (1976): 505–16.

———. "Proportion and Value in Johnson's *Lives of the Poets.*" *South Atlantic Bulletin* 43 (Jan. 1978): 49–57.

Brink, J.R. "Johnson and Milton." *Studies in English Literature* 20 (1980): 493–503.

Burke, John J., Jr. "Excellence in Biography: *Rambler* No. 60 and Johnson's Early Biographies." *South Atlantic Bulletin* 44 (May 1979): 14–34.

Byrd, Max. "Johnson's Spiritual Anxiety." *Modern Philology* 78, No. 4 (May 1981): 368–78.

Campbell, Hilbert H. "Shiels and Johnson: Biographers of Thomson." *Studies in English Literature* 12 (1972): 535–44.

Cohen, Michael M. "The Enchained Heart and the Puzzled Biographer: Johnson's *Life of Savage.*" *New Rambler* 18 (1977): 33–40.

Damrosch, Leopold, Jr. *The Uses of Johnson's Criticism.* Charlottesville: Univ. Press of Virginia, 1976.

Davidson, Virginia Spencer. "Johnson's *Life of Savage*: The Transformation of a Genre." In *Studies in Biography*, ed. Daniel Aaron. Harvard English Studies 8. Cambridge: Harvard Univ. Press, 1978.

DeMaria, Robert Jr. "Johnson's Form of Evaluation." *Studies in English Literature* 19 (1979): 501–14.

Dussinger, John A. "Style and Intention in Johnson's *Life of Savage.*" *ELH* 37 (1970): 564–81.

Edinger, William. *Samuel Johnson and Poetic Style*. Chicago: Univ. of Chicago Press, 1977.

Ellis, Frank H. "Johnson and Savage: Two Failed Tragedies and a Failed Tragic Hero." In *The Author in His Work: Essays on a Problem in Criticism*, ed. Louis L. Martz and Aubrey Williams. New Haven: Yale Univ. Press, 1978.

Fix, Stephen. "Distant Genius: Johnson and the Art of Milton's Life." *Modern Philology* 81, no. 3 (Feb. 1984): 244–64.

Folkenflik, Robert. "Johnson's Art of Anecdote." In *Racism in the Eighteenth Century*, ed. Harold E. Pagliaro. Cleveland: Western Reserve Univ. Press, 1973.

———. "Johnson's Heroes." In *The English Hero, 1660–1800*, ed. Robert Folkenflik. Newark: Univ. of Delaware Press, 1982.

———. *Samuel Johnson, Biographer*. Ithaca, N.Y.: Cornell Univ. Press, 1978.

Fussell, Paul. *Samuel Johnson and the Life of Writing*. New York: Harcourt Brace Jovanovich, 1971.

Grundy, Isobel. "Samuel Johnson: A Writer of Lives Looks at Death." *Modern Language Review* 79 (1984): 257–65.

Halsband, Robert. "The 'Penury of English Biography' Before Samuel Johnson." In *Biography in the 18th Century*, ed. John D. Browning. New York: Garland, 1980.

Hanchock, Paul. "The Structure of Johnson's *Lives*: A Possible Source." *Modern Philology* 74, no. 1 (Aug. 1976): 75–77.

Hardy, J.P. *Samuel Johnson: A Critical Study*. London: Routledge and Kegan Paul, 1979.

Hilles, Frederick W. "Dr. Johnson on Swift's Last Years: Some Misconceptions and Distortions." *Philological Quarterly* 54 (1975): 370–79.

Johnson, Samuel. *Early Biographical Writings of Dr. Johnson*. Ed. J.D. Fleeman. Farnborough: Gregg International, 1973.

———. *Life of Savage*. Ed. Clarence Tracy. Oxford: Clarendon Press, 1971.

Johnston, Shirley White. "The Unfurious Critic: Samuel Johnson's Attitude Toward his Contemporaries." *Modern Philology* 77, no. 1 (Aug. 1979): 18–25.

Kaminski, Thomas. "Was Savage 'Thales'?: Johnson's *London* and Biographical Speculation." *Bulletin of Research in the Humanities* 85 (1982): 322–35.

Keener, Frederick M. *The Chain of Becoming: The Philosophical Tale, the Novel, and a Neglected Realism of the Enlightenment*. New York: Columbia Univ. Press, 1983.

Kinkead-Weekes, Mark. "Johnson on 'The Rise of the Novel.' " In

Samuel Johnson: New Critical Essays, ed. Isobel Grundy. London: Vision, 1984.

Kirkley, Harriet. "Johnson's *Life of Pope*: Fact as Fiction." *Wascana Review* 15 (Fall 1980): 69–80.

Korshin, Paul J. "Johnson and the Earl of Orrery." In *Eighteenth-Century Studies in Honor of Donald F. Hyde*, ed. W.H. Bond. New York: Grolier Club, 1970.

———. "Samuel Johnson and Swift: A Study in the Genesis of Literary Opinion." *Philological Quarterly* 48 (1969): 464–78.

Lill, James. "A Lesson in Futurity: Johnson's *Life of Sir Thomas Browne*." *Notre Dame English Journal* 15 (Winter 1983): 39–50.

Lipking, Lawrence. *The Life of the Poet: Beginning and Ending Poetic Careers*. Chicago: Univ. of Chicago Press, 1981.

———. *The Ordering of the Arts in Eighteenth-Century England*. Princeton: Princeton Univ. Press, 1970.

Maner, Martin. "Samuel Johnson's *Lives*: Its 'Nice Doubtfulness.' " *American Imago* 40 (Summer 1983): 145–58.

———. "Satire and Sympathy in Johnson's *Life of Savage*." *Genre* 8 (1975): 107–18.

McCarthy, William. "The Composition of Johnson's *Lives*: A Calendar." *Philological Quarterly* 60 (1981): 53–67.

———. "The Moral Art of Johnson's *Lives*." *Studies in English Literature* 17 (1977): 502–17.

McIntosh, Carey. *The Choice of Life: Samuel Johnson and the World of Fiction*. New Haven: Yale Univ. Press, 1973.

Misenheimer, James B. "Samuel Johnson, Literary Theory, and the Values of Biography." *New Rambler*, supp. (1978): 29–36.

———. "Samuel Johnson's *Life of Savage*: A Survey." *New Rambler* 10 (Spring 1971): 18–26.

Novak, Maximillian E. "Johnson, Dryden, and the Wild Vicissitudes of Taste." In *The Unknown Samuel Johnson*, ed. John J. Burke, Jr., and Donald Kay. Madison: Univ. of Wisconsin Press, 1983.

Parke, Catherine. "Imlac and Autobiography." In *Studies in Eighteenth-Century Culture* 6, ed. Ronald C. Rosbottom. Madison: Univ. of Wisconsin Press, 1977.

Pettit, Henry. "The Making of Croft's Life of Young for Johnson's *Lives of the Poets*." *Philological Quarterly* 54 (1975): 333–39.

Rogers, Pat. "Johnson's *Lives of the Poets* and the Biographic Dictionaries." *Review of English Studies* n.s. 31 (1980): 149–71.

Swearingen, James E. "Johnson's 'Life of Gray.' " *Texas Studies in Language and Literature* 14 (1972): 283–302.

Uphaus, Robert W. "The 'Equipoise' of Johnson's *Life of Savage*." *Studies in Burke and His Time* 17 (1976): 43–54.

Vesterman, William. "Johnson and *The Life of Savage*." *ELH* 36 (1969): 659–78.
Wendorf, Richard. "The Making of Johnson's *Life of Collins*." *Papers of the Bibliographical Society of America* 75 (1980): 95–115.

NOTES

DAVID WHEELER

Introduction: The Uses of Johnson's Biographies

1. John J. Burke, Jr., *The Unknown Samuel Johnson*, ed. John J. Burke, Jr., and Donald Kay (Madison: Univ. of Wisconsin Press, 1983), 3.

2. Granted, Johnson's numerous biographies are not particularly accessible to the general modern reader. Even students may have some difficulty laying hands on them, for, as William Siebenschuh points out in one of the essays that follow, student editions generally contain Johnson's biographical writings in bits and pieces. And the standard edition of the *Lives of the Poets*, a bulky three volumes, is sure to intimidate students, as might Fleeman's facsimile edition of the early biographies.

3. Samuel Johnson, *The Rambler*, ed. W.J. Bate and Albrecht Strauss, vols. 3-5 of *The Yale Edition of the Works of Samuel Johnson* (New Haven: Yale Univ. Press, 1969), 3:319.

4. Walter Jackson Bate, *Samuel Johnson* (New York: Harcourt Brace Jovanovich, 1977), 220.

5. Ibid., 223.

6. Johnson, *The Rambler*, 3:321.

7. Lawrence Lipking, *The Ordering of the Arts in Eighteenth-Century England* (Princeton: Princeton Univ. Press, 1970), 405.

8. Richard B. Schwartz, *Boswell's Johnson: A Preface to the Life* (Madison: Univ. of Wisconsin Press, 1978), 8.

9. For a good synopsis of these arguments, consult John Vance's collection, *Boswell's Life of Johnson: New Questions, New Answers* (Athens: Univ. of Georgia Press, 1985). Vance's ingenious arrangement of these essays provides a dramatic unfolding of the controversies.

10. Ralph Rader, "Literary Form in Factual Narrative: The Example of Boswell's *Johnson*," in Vance, *Boswell's Life of Johnson*, 32–33.

11. Some of the important source studies not mentioned here are Charles Batten, Jr., "Samuel Johnson's Sources for 'The Life of Roscommon,' " *Modern Philology* 72 (1974): 185–89; James L. Battersby, "Johnson and Shiels: Biographers of Addison," *Studies in English Literature* 9 (1969): 521–37; Benjamin Boyce, "Johnson's *Life of Savage* and Its Literary Background," *Studies in Philology* 53 (1956): 576–98; Benjamin Boyce, "Samuel Johnson's Criticism of Pope in *The Life of Pope*," *Review of English Studies*, n.s. 5 (1954): 37–46; Edward Hart, "Some New Sources of Johnson's *Lives*," *PMLA* 65 (1950): 1088–1111; Frederick W. Hilles, "The Making of *The Life of Pope*," in his *New Light on Dr. Johnson* (New Haven: Yale Univ. Press, 1959), 257–84; Walter Raleigh, *Six Essays on Johnson* (Oxford: Clarendon Press, 1910); and Richard Wendorf, "The Making of Johnson's *Life of Collins*," *Papers of the Bibliographical Society of America* 75 (1980): 95–115.

12. Paul Hanchock, "The Structure of Johnson's *Lives*: A Possible Source," *Modern Philology* 74 (1976): 75–77; Pat Rogers, "Johnson's *Lives of the Poets* and the Biographic Dictionaries," *Review of English Studies*, n.s. 31 (1980): 149–71.

13. Robert Folkenflik, in *Samuel Johnson, Biographer* (Ithaca, N.Y.: Cornell Univ. Press, 1978), the only book-length study of Johnson as a biographer, devotes considerable space to these issues.

LAWRENCE LIPKING

Johnson's Beginnings

1. Donald Greene supplies this translation, along with the Latin text, in his edition of selected works, *Samuel Johnson* (Oxford: Oxford Univ. Press, 1984), 39.

2. Edmund Hector's note to Boswell, in *Correspondence and Other Papers Relating to the Making of the Life of Johnson*, ed. Marshall Waingrow, vol. 2 of the *Yale Editions of the Private Papers of James Boswell* (research ed.) (New York: McGraw-Hill, 1969), 48.

3. Bate, *Samuel Johnson*, 111.

4. Johnson's own phrase, according to Arthur Murphy: *Johnsonian Miscellanies*, ed. George Birkbeck Hill, 2 vols. (Oxford: Clarendon, 1897) 1:467.

5. Samuel Johnson, *Lives of the English Poets*, ed. George Birkbeck Hill, 3 vols. (Oxford: Clarendon, 1905), 2:83.

6. Hill, *Johnsonian Miscellanies*, 1:283.

7. Johnson, *The Rambler*, 5:319.

8. James T. Boulton, ed., *Johnson: The Critical Heritage* (London: Routledge and Kegan Paul, 1971), 355.

9. James Boswell, *Boswell's Life of Johnson*, ed. George Birkbeck Hill, rev. L.F. Powell, 6 vols. (Oxford: Clarendon, 1934–50), 3:174.

10. Johnson, *Lives of the English Poets*, 3:52.

11. Boulton, *Critical Heritage*, 347–48.

12. Johnson, *Lives of the English Poets*, 2:149.

13. Hill, *Johnsonian Miscellanies*, 1:233.

14. Joseph Addison, *Spectator* 303 (16 Feb. 1712).

JAMES L. BATTERSBY

Life, Art, and the *Lives of the Poets*

1. Denis Donoghue, "The Man Who Suffers, the Mind That Creates," *New York Times Book Review*, 11 March 1984, 33.

2. *Oxford English Dictionary*, compact ed., s.v. "character."

3. Richard D. Altick, *Lives and Letters: A History of Literary Biography in England and America* (New York: Knopf, 1965), 57.

4. Ibid., 56–57.

5. See *Boswell's Life*, 1:292.

6. Donoghue, "The Man Who Suffers," 32.

7. Johnson, *Lives of the English Poets*, 1:70, 201.

8. *The Letters of Samuel Johnson*, ed. R.W. Chapman, 3 vols. (Oxford: Clarendon, 1952), 2:340.

9. Johnson may have omitted the anecdotes about Gray that William Cole, a friend of many years, submitted, not simply because he was "weary of his labours and anxious to complete his task," as Courtney and Smith suggest, but also because they contained inert facts, particulars lacking resonance and significance. See William Prideaux Courtney and David Nichol Smith, *A Bibliography of Samuel Johnson* (1925; repr., Oxford: Clarendon, 1968), 132.

10. Samuel Johnson, *Diaries, Prayers, and Annals*, ed., E.L. McAdam, with Donald and Mary Hyde, vol. 1 of *The Yale Edition of the Works of Samuel Johnson* (New Haven: Yale Univ. Press, 1958), 303–4.

11. We know, for example, that when the *Life of Rowe* was turned over to John Nichols for printing, Johnson noted that "the criticism was tolerably well-done, considering that he had not read one of Rowe's plays for thirty years."

12. Johnson, *Preface to Shakespeare*, in *Johnson on Shakespeare*, ed.

Arthur Sherbo, vol. 7 of *The Yale Edition of the Works of Samuel Johnson* (New Haven: Yale Univ. Press, 1968), 71.

13. Bate, *Samuel Johnson*, 530.

14. Lipking, *Ordering of the Arts*, 461.

15. Johnson, *Adventurer* 69, in *Idler and Adventurer*, ed. W.J. Bate, John M. Bullitt, and L.F. Powell, vol. 2 of *The Yale Edition of the Works of Samuel Johnson* (New Haven: Yale Univ. Press, 1963), 394.

16. Of course, the cumulative evidence against Addison is impressive, but it must be remembered that Johnson is the first biographer to accumulate and cite it.

17. For a sense of the importance of the temerity-timidity distinction in Johnson's moral thought, see, for example, *Rambler* 23, 25, 43, 129 and *Adventurer* 69.

18. W.R. Keast, "The Theoretical Foundations of Johnson's Criticism," in *Critics and Criticism: Ancient and Modern*, ed. R.S. Crane (Chicago and London: Univ. of Chicago Press, 1952), 407.

19. Jean H. Hagstrum, *Samuel Johnson's Literary Criticism* (Minneapolis: Univ. of Minnesota Press, 1952), 43.

20. Johnson, *The History of Rasselas, Prince of Abyssinia*, ed. Gwin J. Kolb (New York: Appleton-Century-Crofts, 1962), 65.

21. In Johnson's view, pleasure is a response to the representation or expression of novelty—"novelty is the great source of pleasure" (*Lives* 2:206); variety—"the great source of pleasure is variety" (*Lives* 1:212); or truth—"nothing can please many and please long but just representations of general nature" (*Preface to Shakespeare*, 61).

22. Hagstrum, *Johnson's Literary Criticism*, 43.

23. Folkenflik, *Samuel Johnson, Biographer*, 141.

24. Joseph Wood Krutch, *Samuel Johnson* (1944; repr., New York: Harcourt, Brace and World, 1963), 465.

25. M.H. Abrams, *The Mirror and the Lamp: Romantic Theory and the Critical Tradition* (1953; repr., New York: Norton, 1958), 233–34.

26. Hagstrum, *Johnson's Literary Criticism*, 46–47.

27. Lipking, *Ordering of the Arts*, 438.

28. Ibid., 420.

29. Leopold Damrosch, Jr., *The Uses of Johnson's Criticism* (Charlottesville: Univ. Press of Virginia, 1976), 126.

30. For further consideration of the issue and for those passages in Johnson's writings especially relevant to it, see Folkenflik, *Samuel Johnson, Biographer*, chaps. 6, 7.

31. Ibid., 116.

32. Johnson, *The Rambler*, 3:74.

33. Occasionally, Johnson does practice technical and formal criticism, as when, for example, he deals with the adequacy of image to

thought in particular poems, or with particular matters of prosody or rhyme; or when he takes up seriatim, in conventional fashion, fable, character, diction, etc., or considers the probability of actions; but usually, even when he appears to be most deeply engaged in the nitty-gritty of "professional" criticism, he is making more or less audible references to characteristic genius or to comparative achievement.

34. Lipking, *Ordering of the Arts*, 460.

35. Wayne C. Booth, *Critical Understanding: The Powers and Limits of Pluralism* (Chicago: Univ. of Chicago Press, 1979), 268–72.

36. Booth, *Critical Understanding*, 268.

37. Folkenflik, *Samuel Johnson, Biographer*, 123.

38. Booth, *Critical Understanding*, 269.

39. Ibid.

40. Notice, for example, how differently Johnson handles gorgeously inflated praise when it is proffered by Dryden and when it is directed to Halifax—"very near to admiration is the wish to admire" (*Lives* 2:47).

41. To substantiate his perception of the implications of Pope's letters, Johnson goes to a variety of "external" sources, mostly other writings, thereby validating subtext by text.

42. Booth, *Critical Understanding*, 270.

43. Johnson, *A Journey to the Western Islands of Scotland*, ed. Mary Lascelles, vol. 9 of *The Yale Edition of the Works of Samuel Johnson* (New Haven: Yale Univ. Press, 1971), 40.

44. Folkenflik, *Samuel Johnson, Biographer*, 144.

45. Folkenflik notes that "one-quarter of the *Lives of the Poets* contain no personal characters." See ibid., 102.

46. Altick, *Lives and Letters*, 57.

47. Ibid.

48. See, for example, Michael Polanyi, *The Tacit Dimension* (Garden City, N.Y.: Doubleday, 1966), chap. 1.

49. Booth, *Critical Understanding*, 317–18.

50. *Boswell's Life* 4:421. These quoted remarks are taken from the passage at the end of the *Life*, in which Boswell cites the response of William Gerard Hamilton to Johnson's death.

JOHN A. DUSSINGER

Dr. Johnson's Solemn Response to Beneficence

1. Samuel Johnson, *Life of Savage*, ed. Clarence Tracy (Oxford: Clarendon, 1971), 40. Subsequent citations by page number in the text of the essay are to this edition.

2. Lucien Goldmann, *The Philosophy of the Enlightenment: The Christian Burgess and the Enlightenment* (London: Routledge and Kegan Paul, 1968), 63.

3. "It is a duty to give to the poor; but no man can say how much another should give to the poor, or when a man has given too little to save his soul" (*Boswell's Life* 2:250).

4. Jane Austen, *Emma*, ed. R.W. Chapman (London: Oxford Univ. Press, 1960), 87.

5. *Boswell's Life* 4:321–22.

6. *Boswell's Life* 1:83–84. Like Boswell, Mrs. Piozzi looked in bewilderment upon Johnson's tireless charity. "He nursed whole nests of people in his house, where the lame, the blind, the sick, and the sorrowful found a sure retreat from all the evils whence his little income could secure them . . . treating them with the same, or perhaps more ceremonious civility, than he would have done by as many people of fashion—making the holy scriptures thus the rule of his conduct and only expecting salvation as he was able to obey its precepts" (Hill, *Johnsonian Miscellanies*, 1:205).

7. Johnson, *Diaries, Prayers, and Annals*, 369.

8. Mrs. Piozzi, in Hill, *Johnsonian Miscellanies* 1:204.

9. Samuel Johnson, *Life of Addison*, in *Lives of the English Poets*, 2:97.

10. Paul Kent Alkon, *Samuel Johnson and Moral Discipline* (Evanston: Northwestern Univ. Press, 1967), 27.

11. Ibid., 34–35, 61.

12. Mrs. Piozzi, in Hill, *Johnsonian Miscellanies* 1:205.

13. Johnson, *Life of Addison*, in *Lives of the English Poets*, 2:123.

14. *Boswell's Life* 1:169–70.

15. Ibid., 1:173n.

16. Ibid., 3:188–89. Quoting from the notes of the Reverend Dr. Maxwell, Boswell records Johnson's opinions on rank. "Though of no high extraction himself, he had much respect for birth and family, especially among ladies. He said, 'adventitious accomplishments may be possessed by all ranks; but one may easily distinguish the *born gentleman!* '" (Ibid., 2:130).

17. Ibid., 1:77

18. Ibid., 164.

19. Samuel Johnson, *A Dictionary of the English Language*, facsimile ed. (London: Times Books, 1979), s.v. "patron."

20. Mrs. Piozzi, in Hill, *Johnsonian Miscellanies* 1:206.

21. *Boswell's Life* 2:10.

22. Alkon, *Johnson and Moral Discipline*, 53.

23. Quoted in E. Allison Peers, *Spirit of Flame: A Study of St. John of the Cross* (London: Student Christian Movement Press, 1943), 97.

24. Alkon, *Johnson and Moral Discipline*, 54.

25. Frederick M. Keener, *The Chain of Becoming: The Philosophical Tale, the Novel, and a Neglected Realism of the Enlightenment* (New York: Columbia Univ. Press, 1983), 55–85.

26. Joseph Burroughs, *The Blessedness of a Benevolent Temper: A Sermon preached at the Old Jewry, March 2d. 1742, to the Society for Relief of the Widows and Orphans of Protestant Dissenting Ministers* (London, 1743), 14.

27. Johnson, *The Rambler*, 5:116. The translation is by Edward Cave.

28. Thomas Hobbes, *Leviathan, or The Matter, Form, and Power of a Commonwealth Ecclesiastical and Civil*, vol. 3 of *The English Works*, ed. Sir William Molesworth, 11 vols. (London: John Bohn, 1839), 87.

29. "A droll little circumstance once occurred: As if he meant to reprimand my minute exactness as a creditor, he thus addressed me;—'Boswell, *lend* me sixpence—*not to be repaid*' " (*Boswell's Life*, 4:191).

30. Hobbes, *Leviathan* 88.

JAMES GRAY

Johnson's Portraits of Charles XII of Sweden

1. Samuel Johnson, *Poems*, ed. E.L. McAdam, Jr., with George Milne, vol. 6 of *The Yale Edition of the Works of Samuel Johnson* (New Haven: Yale Univ. Press, 1964), 101–2.

2. For a discussion of Johnson's "sombre" and "stern" treatment of Charles XII, in contrast to Juvenal's "spiteful" attack on the vainglorious Hannibal, see Mary Lascelles, "Johnson and Juvenal," in *Notions and Facts* (Oxford: Clarendon, 1972), 146–48.

3. See Daniel Defoe, *A Short View of the Conduct of the King of Sweden*, (London, 1716); *A History of the Wars of His Present Majesty Charles XII by a Scots Gentleman in the Swedish Service* (London, 1715; 2d ed., 1720); and *What If the Swedes Should Come?* (London, 1717). The last of these, only conjecturally attributed to Defoe, was written in response to threats and rumors that Charles was planning an invasion of Britain to support the Jacobite cause. For Defoe's comments on Charles XII in his *Review*, see Walter Wilson, *Memoirs of the Life and Times of Daniel Defoe*, 3 vols. (London: Hurst, Chance, 1830),

2:519–20; 3:116. Johnson had compiled a catalogue of Defoe's writings, of which he held a high opinion. See *Boswell's Life* 3:267–68.

4. Voltaire, *History of Charles XII, King of Sweden*, 4th ed. (London, 1732). For the purpose of this essay, this translation has been consulted. The *History* is in eight books, of which the last two were translated by John Locker (1693–1760). Andrew Henderson, the main translator, whose birth and death dates are uncertain, published in 1775 two letters attacking Johnson and his *Journey to the Western Islands of Scotland. DNB* describes him as a well-read but eccentric character. The names of the translators do not appear on the title page of the *History*.

5. Hill, *Johnsonian Miscellanies* 2:306. On other occasions Johnson was quite critical of Voltaire as a historian, contending that his honesty was not equal to his knowledge; that his imagination sometimes outran his information as it caught "greedily at wonders"; that he so much loved a striking story that "he told what he could not find to be true"; and so on. Yet he commended Voltaire's methods in collecting materials for his *History of Louis XIV*, noting that "his principal merit consisted in a happy selection and arrangement of circumstances" (Joseph Epes Brown, *Critical Opinions of Samuel Johnson* [1926; repr., New York: Russell and Russell, 1961], 532–33). For Johnson's rather negative opinions about historians in general, see *Rambler* 122; *Idler* 84; *Boswell's Life* 1:424–25; 2:365–66; 5:403. In *Rambler* 122 he deplores the paucity of good English historians, though he has some praise for Clarendon and more for Knolles. As this *Rambler* was written less than a year after the Drury Lane performance of *Mahomet and Irene*, it has an obvious connecting interest.

6. Henry Fielding, *Amelia*, ed. Martin C. Battestin, in *The Wesleyan Edition of the Works of Henry Fielding* (New York: Oxford Univ. Press, 1983), 130 and n.

7. See Jerry C. Beasley, *Novels of the 1740s* (Athens: Univ. of Georgia Press, 1982), 177–79.

8. Chesterfield to his godson, *French Correspondence of the Earl of Chesterfield*, ed. Rex A. Barrell, 2 vols. (Ottawa: Borealis, 1980), 2:83 (letter 218); 2:89 (letter 224).

9. Chesterfield to Voltaire, 27 Aug. 1752, *French Correspondence* 1:135 (letter 98).

10. Chesterfield to his son, 4 Oct. 1752, *Letters Written by the Earl of Chesterfield to His Son*, 5th ed., 4 vols. (London: Eugenia Stanhope, 1774), 3:372 (letter 259).

11. Folkenflik, *Samuel Johnson, Biographer*, 64–69; Johnson, *Lives of the English Poets* 3:200.

12. See, e.g., Johnson's "Thoughts on . . . Falkland's Islands" (1771),

where he paints a grim picture of the life of the modern soldier and attacks warmongers and war profiteers. *Political Writings*, ed. Donald J. Greene, vol. 10 of *The Yale Edition of the Works of Samuel Johnson* (New Haven: Yale Univ. Press, 1977), 370–76.

13. See Johnson, "The Bravery of the English Common Soldiers," in *Political Writings*, 281–84.

14. See Mary Alden Hopkins, *Dr. Johnson's Lichfield* (New York: Hastings, 1952), 7–10, 49.

15. Hopkins, *Johnson's Lichfield*, 232; Carola Oman, *David Garrick* (London: Hodder and Stoughton, 1958), 11; David Erskine Baker, *Biographia Dramatica*, 2 vols. (London, 1782), 2:300; Mary E. Knapp, *Prologues and Epilogues of the Eighteenth Century* (New Haven: Yale Univ. Press, 1961), 214.

16. *Boswell's Life* 3:265–66. For Johnson's visit to Warley Camp, when Bennet Langton was a captain in the Lincolnshire Militia, see ibid., 360–62; and for Johnson's own service in the militia, see ibid. 4:319. Unfortunately, we have no record of the time or nature of that service, but Boswell reports seeing "a musket, with sword and belt," hanging in Johnson's closet. For further favorable comments on soldiers and officers, see ibid. 3:9-10.

17. Ibid. 2:475 and n. 3; Voltaire, *History of Charles XII*, 87, 130.

18. *The Letters of Samuel Johnson*, ed. R.W. Chapman, 3 vols. (Oxford: Clarendon, 1952), 1:14–15 (letter 15); 1:15–17 (letter 17 and n. 3). The dating of letter 17 is based, presumably, on Johnson's reference to Frederick the Great's peace treaty with Hungary, and Cartaret's involvement in foreign policy. Since Cartaret succeeded Robert Walpole in February 1742, there is a good prima facie case for a date later than that; but the Peace of Berlin, to which Johnson appears to be referring, was not signed until July 1743. It is true, however, that Frederick had made two previous gestures of peace toward Maria Theresa, in October 1741, and July 1742, and references to the second of these appeared in the *Gentleman's Magazine* (July 1742), 389.

19. See James Gray, "*Mahomet and Irene:* More Tragedy than Triumph," *Humanities Association Review* 27 (1976): 422–40; 28 (1977): 65–87.

20. Stonehouse to Garrick, *The Letters of David Garrick*, ed. David M. Little and George M. Kahrl, 3 vols. (London: Oxford Univ. Press, 1963), 3:1356 (app. D).

21. Count Johan Reinhold Patkul, a native of Livonia (a former Russian province on the Baltic and now part of the Latvian and Estonian republics of the Soviet Union), bore a bitter grudge against the Swedish government for having confiscated his estate, together with the patrimonies of many of his fellow countrymen. Deputed by

the nobility of Livonia to protest this treatment, he addressed Charles's predecessor, Charles XI, in forthright terms, and was subsequently condemned to death for high treason. Patkul escaped to Poland, where he elicited the support of King Augustus, who laid siege to the capital of Livonia, Riga, in 1700, but failed to capture it. Patkul, one of the two commanders at the siege, was later promoted to the rank of general. Then he entered the service of Moscow, and acted as the tsar's ambassador to several countries. Charles XII, however, ignoring Patkul's diplomatic status and considering him a deserter from the Swedish Empire, as well as a traitor, had him seized and imprisoned in 1707, when he was condemned to be broken alive on the wheel, and then quartered, thus discharging the sentence that had been pronounced by Charles XI. A modern historian has called Patkul "the prime mover in the undoing of Sweden . . . who wove the network of a war coalition" (Saxony, Russia, Poland, Denmark) which was eventually to "bring the Swedish Empire toppling to the ground" (Herbert Albert Laurens Fisher, *A History of Europe* [London: E. Arnold, 1937], 710).

22. *Memoirs of Percival Stockdale*, 2 vols. (London, 1809); quoted in James Boswell, *The Life of Samuel Johnson*, ed. John Wilson Croker, rev. John Wright, 10 vols. (London: Bohn, 1859), 10:53.

23. Robert Nisbet Bain, *Charles XII and the Collapse of the Swedish Empire, 1682–1719* (1895; repr., Freeport, N.Y.: Books for Libraries Press, 1969), 312.

24. Ibid., 312–14.

25. Ragnhild Marie Hatton, *Charles XII of Sweden* (New York: Weybright and Talley, 1968), 311–12.

26. Reprinted in Voltaire, *The History of Charles the Twelfth, King of Sweden* (Hartford, Conn.: Andrus and Judd, 1833), 8–9.

27. Ibid., 274. The earlier translation reads: "Of all his old opinions he retained but one, which was absolute predestination, a doctrine that favour'd his courage, and justified his rash adventures" (Voltaire, *History of Charles XII* [London, 1732], 365).

28. Hatton, *Charles XII*, 431–32.

29. Samuel Johnson, *The Idler and the Adventurer*, 432–33. It should be noted that, in his article on Charles Frederick, King of Prussia, first published in the *Literary Magazine* for 1756, Johnson appears to excuse Charles XII to some extent by implying that Peter the Great's motive in attacking him was the result of personal peeve. See *The Works of Samuel Johnson*, ed. F.P. Walesby, 9 vols. (Oxford: Talboys and Wheeler, 1825), 6:464.

30. Johnson to Thrale, 10 April 1778, *Letters*, 2:260–61 (letter 585.1). Johnson was interested in going to Sweden and meeting

Charles XII's descendant, King Gustavus III, who had expressed the opinion that his predecessor "was rather extraordinary than great. He certainly had not the true conquering temperament which simply aims at acquisition of territory. Charles took dominions with one hand only to give them away with the other. Superior to Alexander, with whom it were an injustice to compare him, he was as much inferior to hs rival Peter in the qualities which make him a great ruler, as he excelled him in those qualities which go to make him a great hero" (quoted in Bain, *Charles XII*, 314). Boswell (three of whose ancestors had gone to Sweden in the seventeenth century to fight in Gustavus Adolphus' wars) first proposed the project of "our going to the Baltick" and seeing the king of Sweden when he and Johnson were in Skye (*Boswell's Life* 5:215). Johnson appeared eager to go, but Boswell, much to his later regret, decided against the scheme. Gustavus III was assassinated in 1792. See *Boswell's Life* 2:288 and n.; 3:134 and n.; Johnson, *Letters* 1:416 (letter 363); James Boswell, *Journal of a Tour to the Hebrides*, ed. F.A. Pottle and C.H. Bennett (New York: Viking, 1936), 175; *The Ominous Years, 1774–1776*, ed. C. Ryskamp and F.A. Pottle, *The Yale Editions of the Private Papers of James Boswell* (New York: McGraw-Hill, 1963), 211 and n.

CATHERINE N. PARKE

Johnson, Imlac, and Biographical Thinking

1. Samuel Johnson, *Lives of the English Poets*, ed. George Birkbeck Hill, 3 vols. (Oxford: Clarendon, 1905), 1:454. Subsequent citations by volume and page number in the text of the essay are to this edition.

2. For a book-length exploration of conversation as one of the possible aims of knowledge, see Richard Rorty, *Philosophy and the Mirror of Nature* (Princeton: Princeton Univ. Press, 1979). In the essay "*Rasselas* and the Conversation of History" in *The Age of Johnson*, ed. Paul J. Korshin, forthcoming (New York: AMS Press, 1987), I elaborate this discussion of conversation as Johnson's model for historiography.

3. This characterization of the proofs of probability is taken from Hoyt Trowbridge's essay on Johnson and the "ethos" of probabilism: "Scattered Atoms of Probability," *Eighteenth-Century Studies* 5 (Fall 1971): 16.

4. Samuel Johnson, *Early Biographical Writings of Dr. Johnson*, ed. J.D. Fleeman (Farnborough: Gregg International, 1973), 417.

5. All who write about *Rasselas* owe a general debt to the broadly intelligent and nuanced history of its critical studies that date es-

pecially from the 1950s. Among these I would give especial note to Mary Lascelles, "*Rasselas* Reconsidered," *Essays and Studies by Members of the English Association*, n.s. 4 (1951): 37–52; Gwin J. Kolb, "The Structure of *Rasselas*," *PMLA* 66 (1951): 698–717; Alvin Whitley, "The Comedy of Rasselas," *ELH* 23 (1956): 48–70; Frederick M. Link, "Rasselas and the Quest for Happiness," *Boston University Studies in English* 3 (Summer 1957): 121–23; Nicholas Joost, "Whispers of Fancy; or, the Meaning of *Rasselas*," *Modern Age* 1 (Fall 1957): 166–73; Geoffrey Tillotson, "Time in *Rasselas*," in *Bicentenary Essays on Rasselas*, ed. Magdi Wahba, supplement to *Cairo Studies in English* (Cairo, 1959), 97–103; W.K. Wimsatt, "In Praise of *Rasselas:* Four Notes (Converging)," in *Imagined Worlds: Essays on Some English Novels and Novelists in Honor of John Butt*, ed. Maynard Mack and Ian Gregor (London: Methuen, 1968), 111–36; Carey McIntosh, *The Choice of Life: Samuel Johnson and the World of Fiction* (New Haven: Yale Univ. Press, 1973), esp. 163–213; Patrick O'Flaherty, "Dr. Johnson as Equivocator: The Meaning of *Rasselas*," *Modern Language Quarterly* 31 (1970): 195–206; Gloria Sybil Gross, "Sanity, Madness, and the Family in Samuel Johnson's *Rasselas*," *Psychocultural Review* 1 (1977): 152–59; Irvin Ehrenpreis, "*Rasselas* and Some Meanings of 'Structure' in Literary Criticism," *Novel* 14 (1984): 101–17; Edward Tomarken, "Travels into the Unknown: *Rasselas* and *A Journey to the Western Islands*," in Burke and Kay, *Unknown Samuel Johnson*, 150–65.

6. Samuel Johnson, *The History of Rasselas Prince of Abissinia*, ed. Geoffrey Tillotson and Brian Jenkins (London: Oxford Univ. Press, 1971), 61. Subsequent citations by page number in the text of the essay are to this edition.

7. In an essay, "Imlac and Autobiography," in *Studies in Eighteenth-Century Culture* 6, ed. Ronald C. Rosbottom (Madison: Univ. of Wisconsin Press, 1977), 183–96, I have discussed Imlac as a model teacher.

8. These are Nietzsche's categories of historical investigation proposed in *The Use and Abuse of History*, trans. Adrian Collins (Indianapolis: Bobbs-Merrill, 1949), 3, 12, 14.

9. Kenneth Burke discusses this conception of inheritance in *Attitudes Toward History* (Boston: Beacon, 1961), 125.

10. These observations bear a family resemblance to Walter Jackson Bate's conception of Johnson's "satire *manqué*," developed in his essay "Johnson and Satire *Manqué*," in *Eighteenth-Century Studies in Honor of Donald F. Hyde*, ed. W.H. Bond (New York: Grolier Club, 1970), 145–60. Bate proposes that Johnson never fails finally to implicate himself in the condition of error that he satirizes. The difference

between Bate's and my approach to this matter lies in where our respective accents fall. Bate uses the ethical imperative to frame the philosophical, whereas I use the philosophical or epistemological to frame the ethical.

STEPHEN FIX

The Contexts and Motives of Johnson's *Life of Milton*

1. Johnson, *Poems*, 240.

2. Johnson, *Lives of the English Poets*, ed. George Birkbeck Hill, 3 vols. (Oxford: Clarendon, 1905), 1:194. Subsequent citations to the *Life of Milton* (1:84–200) are cited by page number only in the text of the essay.

3. As T.S. Eliot observed: "It is a pity that what the common reader today has read, or has remembered, or has seen quoted, are mostly . . . statements of Johnson's [about Milton] from which later critics have vehemently dissented" ("Milton II," in *On Poetry and Poets* [New York: Farrar, Straus, and Cudahy, 1957], 167).

4. For a fuller discussion of the importance of this "integrity" in Johnson's view of Milton, and especially of *Paradise Lost*, see my essays: "Distant Genius: Johnson and the Art of Milton's Life," *Modern Philology* 81, no. 3 (Feb. 1984): 244–64; and "Johnson and the 'Duty' of Reading *Paradise Lost*," *ELH* 52 (1985): 649–71.

5. Johnson, *The Rambler* 4:87–89 (*Rambler* 86).

6. Ibid., 99 (*Rambler* 88).

7. Ibid., 93 (*Rambler* 86).

8. Ibid., 376–77 (*Rambler* 140).

9. Ibid., 383 (*Rambler* 140).

10. Milton was the first major English writer whose biography was written by people who actually knew and were friendly with him. Johnson may well believe that Milton's early biographers were too much Milton's partisans to record his life objectively and dispassionately. Johnson is particularly sensitive to the effects of friendship on biography and criticism. In several Lives, Johnson dismisses earlier biographies because they were written by friends of the writers. See, for example, the opening of the *Life of Cowley (Lives of the Poets* 1:1). Johnson's one-hundred-year test of literary durability, elaborated in his criticism of Shakespeare, is predicated on the assumption that a man's reputation can be justly assessed only after friends and foes alike are dead. Johnson writes the *Life of Milton* slightly more than one hundred years after Milton's death.

11. Ibid. 2:147.

12. For more about Milton's reputation in the eighteenth century and his importance for its writers, see R.D. Havens, *The Influence of Milton on English Poetry* (Cambridge: Harvard Univ. Press, 1922); Walter Jackson Bate, *The Burden of the Past and the English Poet* (Cambridge: Harvard Univ. Press, 1970); Ants Oras, *Milton's Editors and Commentators from Patrick Hume to Henry John Todd (1695–1801): A Study in Critical Views and Methods* (London: Oxford Univ. Press, 1931). The context in which Johnson writes about Milton was created not by critics and biographers alone, but by poets as well. Johnson clearly is displeased by the widespread imitation of Milton he sees in contemporary poetry. See, for example, *Lives of the English Poets* 3:316–20. Johnson may hope that his criticism, by showing the true nature of Milton's talents, would discourage certain kinds of imitations, especially pastorals.

13. Johnson, *The Rambler* 4:102 (*Rambler* 88).

14. Johnson, *Johnson on Shakespeare*, 7:54. For another example of this view, see *The Rambler* 5:78–79 *(Rambler* 158). For Johnson's remarks on the "superficiality" of Addison's commentary on *Paradise Lost*, see *Lives of the English Poets* 2:146–47.

15. Quoted in Malone to Lord Charlemont, 5 April 1779, in Hill, *Johnsonian Miscellanies* 1:483.

16. Ibid. 1:264. When discussing all kinds of praise, Johnson apparently was very fond of (or Mrs. Thrale very attentive to) strangulation metaphors. Thrale reports that Johnson "once bade a very celebrated lady, who praised him with too much zeal perhaps, or perhaps too strong an emphasis (which always offended him), 'consider what her flattery was worth before she choked him with it' " (Ibid. 1:273).

17. Quotations from Richardson's *Life of Milton* are from *The Early Lives of Milton*, ed. Helen Darbishire (London: Constable, 1932), 285, 254.

18. For the views of other Romantic artists and critics on Milton, and on Johnson's *Life of Milton*, see Joseph Anthony Wittreich, Jr., ed., *The Romantics on Milton: Formal Essays and Critical Asides*, (Cleveland: Case Western Reserve Univ. Press, 1970). Wittreich's introduction also provides interesting commentary on the Romantic reaction to Johnson's views.

19. William Hayley, *Life of Milton*, 2d ed. (London, 1796), 229. Hayley's work has been reprinted in a facsimile edition by Wittreich (Gainesville, Fla.: Scholars' Facsimiles, 1970).

20. Ibid., xi.

21. Ibid., xvii, 219, 230.

22. Ibid., 242.

23. Johnson, *The Rambler* 4:122 (*Rambler* 92).

24. *Boswell's Life*, 4:81–82.

25. For more detailed studies of the Lauder affair, see Michael Marcuse, "Miltonoklastes: The Lauder Affair Reconsidered," *Eighteenth-Century Life* 4 (1978): 86–91; Marcuse, "The Pre–Publication History of William Lauder's *Essay on Milton's Use and Imitation of the Moderns in his Paradise Lost*," *Papers of the Bibliographical Society of America* 72 (1978): 35–57; James L. Clifford, "Johnson and Lauder," *Philological Quarterly* 54 (1975): 342–56; Clifford, *Dictionary Johnson: Samuel Johnson's Middle Years* (New York: McGraw-Hill, 1979), esp. 57–70; Warren Mild, "Johnson and Lauder: A Reexamination," *Modern Language Quarterly* 14 (1953): 149–53; Lloyd Lacy, "Samuel Johnson and William Lauder: Malevolence in the Criticism of Milton," *New Rambler*, ser. C, 7 (June 1969): 38–44. The most thorough and conclusive studies are those by Marcuse in *PBSA* and Clifford in *PQ*.

26. William Lauder, *An Essay on Milton's Use and Imitation of the Moderns in his Paradise Lost* (1750; repr., New York: AMS Press, 1973), 151.

27. Havens, *Influence of Milton*, 30.

28. Douglas's discoveries were published in his book, *Milton No Plagiary; or, A Detection of the Forgeries Contained in Lauder's Essay on the Imitation of the Moderns in the Paradise Lost* (London, 1751).

29. Joseph Towers, *An Essay On the Life, Character, and Writings of Dr. Samuel Johnson* (London, 1786) in O.M. Brack, Jr. and Robert E. Kelley, eds., *The Early Biographies of Samuel Johnson* (Iowa City: Univ. of Iowa Press, 1974), 203.

30. Johnson, in *Gentleman's Magazine* 17 (Aug. 1747): 404.

31. Ibid.

32. Ibid.

33. Boswell would later appreciate the irony of his own interest in cataloguing Johnson's houses, and of Johnson's unexpected cooperation in his effort. But the differences in the situations, from Johnson's probable viewpoint, are instructive. In giving such information to Boswell, Johnson probably thought he was supplying material for the most useful kind of literature, biography. But he may have thought (with mildly self-serving inconsistency) that in reproducing the same information about Milton, biographers were not adding significantly to public understanding of Milton, but were instead promoting his legend. See *Boswell's Life* 1:111; 3:405.

34. For another example of Johnson's impatience with such stories, see *Lives of the English Poets* 1:158–59.

35. Johnson, *The Rambler* 4:376 (*Rambler* 139).

36. Joseph Warton is the writer here. He is paraphrasing and endorsing the views of Fenton. Quoted in *The Poetical Works of John Milton*, ed. Henry John Todd (London, 1801), 5:51. This variorum edition is perhaps the most convenient sourcebook for eighteenth-century critical views on Milton. See also George Sherburn, "The Early Popularity of Milton's Minor Poems," *Modern Philology* 17 (1919–20): 259–70, 515–40.

37. Johnson, *Lives of the English Poets* 3:324.

38. Quoted in *Poetical Works of Milton* 5:51.

39. Ibid.

40. In one of the most interesting studies of Johnson's *Lycidas* criticism, Warren Fleischauer minimizes the significance of Johnson's harsh objections to the poem by arguing that it was neither popular nor well known in the eighteenth century, and that up until 1779, *Lycidas* had endured "a century and a half of neglect in the *consensus gentium.*" "The infamous passage from Johnson's *Milton* on 'Lycidas' is the first critique of that poem by a major English literary critic," Fleischauer continues, and we must therefore be careful not to treat his objections to it as a reckless attempt to topple everyone's favorite statue in England's finest museum ("Johnson, 'Lycidas,' and the Norms of Criticism," in *Johnsonian Studies*, ed. Magdi Wahba [Cairo, 1962], 240–41).

Fleischauer's cautions are useful, but his premises and conclusions are not reliable. That Johnson was the first critic to examine *Lycidas* at length does not demonstrate that the poem was unpopular, unknown, or unregarded. Indeed, Johnson's whole critique begins with a notice of the widespread praise and attention *Lycidas* had commanded. Moreover, the major eighteenth-century critics tended to submerge evaluations of individual poems in general critiques of their authors (a practice from which Johnson dissents). The lack of extensive critical debate on *Lycidas* may as easily indicate that it was widely accepted and admired, as that it was ignored. Indeed, the evidence I have cited tends to confirm that the critical situation Johnson confronted was not one of neglect of *Lycidas*, but rather one of careless, enthusiastic admiration.

41. Johnson, *The Rambler* 4:201 (*Rambler* 106).

WILLIAM R. SIEBENSCHUH

Johnson's *Lives* and Modern Students

1. I refer here, of course, not only to the well-known and sustained efforts of professors Donald Greene and Richard Schwartz to correct

what they argue are errors, omissions, and distortions in Boswell's portrait, but also to the works of scholars like Bate, Clifford, Quinlan, Hagstrum, Bronson, and the many others who began, during this period, to deal in depth with aspects of Johnson's life, personality, and literary achievement not covered fully or adequately by Boswell in the *Life of Johnson*.

2. T.S. Eliot, "Johnson As Critic and Poet," in *On Poetry and Poets*, 187.

3. Johnson, *Lives of the English Poets*, ed. George Birkbeck Hill, 3 vols. (Oxford: Clarendon, 1905), 1:21. Subsequent citations in the text of the essay are to this edition.

4. Roland Barthes, "Myth Today," in *A Barthes Reader*, ed. Susan Sontag (New York: Hill and Wang, 1982), 145.

5. Ibid.

6. Martin Duberman, review of *Enlarging the Change*, by Robert Fitzgerald, *New York Times Book Review*, 13 Jan. 1985, 39.

7. John Updike, "Ungreat Lives," review of *Voices From the Moon*, by Andre Dubus, *New Yorker*, 4 Feb. 1985, 97.

8. Eliot, "Johnson As Critic and Poet," 184.

9. *Samuel Johnson: Selected Poetry and Prose*, ed. Frank Brady and W.K. Wimsatt (Berkeley: Univ. of California Press, 1977).

10. Folkenflik, *Samuel Johnson, Biographer*.

11. Hagstrum, *Johnson's Literary Criticism;* Damrosch, *Uses of Johnson's Criticism;* William Edinger, *Samuel Johnson and Poetic Style* (Chicago: Univ. of Chicago Press, 1977).

12. Walter Jackson Bate, *The Achievement of Samuel Johnson* (Chicago: Univ. of Chicago Press, 1978), 171.

13. M.H. Abrams, *The Mirror and the Lamp*, 4.

14. Eliot, "Johnson As Critic and Poet," 192.

15. Ulrich Neisser, *Cognitive Psychology* (New York: Appleton, Century Crofts, 1967), 3.

16. Quoted in Richard M. Restak, *The Brain: The Last Frontier* (New York: Doubleday, 1979), 68–69.

17. Eliot, "Johnson As Critic and Poet," 185.

18. *Boswell's Life* 4:493.

MICHAEL STUPRICH

Johnson and Biography: Recent Critical Directions

1. Predicting exact publication dates is still something of a problem. In a recent letter John H. Middendorf, the general editor of the

Yale series, calls the volumes containing the *Lives of the Poets* "about ⅔ completed." Professor Middendorf, however, makes no mention of the progress on the early biographies. Until their completion, the best available source for the pre-*Lives* biographies is probably the 1825 edition of Johnson's works edited by Robert Lynam. The texts are minimally annotated, but a comparison with Fleeman's reprints shows them to be for the most part reliable.

2. Krutch, *Samuel Johnson*, 82.

3. John J. Burke, Jr., "Excellence in Biography: *Rambler* No. 60 and Johnson's Early Biographies," *South Atlantic Bulletin* 44 (May 1979): 14–34, has an interesting discussion of just exactly what Johnson means by "parallel circumstances and kindred images."

CONTRIBUTORS

JAMES L. BATTERSBY is professor of English at Ohio State University and the author of *Typical Folly: Evaluating Student Performance in Higher Education*; *Rational Praise and Natural Lamentation: Johnson, Lycidas and Principles of Criticism*; *Elder Olson: An Annotated Bibliography*; and of numerous articles on eighteenth-century literature and literary criticism. He is also editing the *Life of Addison* for the *Yale Edition of the Works of Samuel Johnson*.

JOHN DUSSINGER is associate professor of English at the University of Illinois, Urbana-Champaign, where he has taught since receiving his doctorate at Princeton. He has also been a visiting professor in England and Scandinavia. Author of *The Discourse of the Mind in Eighteenth-Century Fiction* and of numerous articles and reviews relating to the period from 1660 to 1820, he has recently completed a book manuscript on Jane Austen's novels.

STEPHEN FIX is dean of the college and associate professor of English at Williams College. He has published articles on Johnson's *Life of Milton* in *ELH* and *Modern Philology* and has presented papers on Johnson at conferences in this country and in England.

JAMES GRAY is Thomas McCulloch Professor of English at Dalhousie University in Halifax, Nova Scotia, Canada. His most recent publications have included monographs and articles on the eighteenth-century theater, Robert Dodsley, Adam Smith, David Garrick, William Dodd, Alexander Pope as translator of the *Odyssey*, and Dr. Johnson's views on authority. His book on the religious writings of Johnson was published by the Clarendon Press in 1972, and he is co-editor, with Jean Hagstrum, of the Yale edition of Johnson's *Sermons*. He is also a member of the editorial board of the *Yale Edition of the Works of Samuel Johnson*.

LAWRENCE LIPKING is Chester D. Tripp Professor of Humanities at Northwestern University. He is the author of *The Ordering of the Arts in Eighteenth-Century England*, *The Life of the Poet* (Christian Gauss Award, 1982), and the forthcoming *Abandoned Women and Poetic Tradition*. The essay in this volume is part of a work in progress on Johnson's career.

CATHERINE N. PARKE is associate professor in the Department of English at the University of Missouri–Columbia, where she is also an associate editor of *The Missouri Review*. She has written on, among others, Jane Austen, James Boswell, Fanny Burney, Samuel Johnson, Sir Joshua Reynolds, and Virginia Woolf. Currently she is at work on a study of Johnson's biographical writings.

WILLIAM SIEBENSCHUH is associate professor of English at Case Western Reserve University and vice dean of Western Reserve College. In addition to numerous essays on Johnson and Boswell, he is the author of *Fictional Techniques and Factual Works* and *Form and Purpose in Boswell's Biographical Works*.

MICHAEL STUPRICH is assistant professor of English at Ithaca College. His recent dissertation is a study of Johnson's early biographies.

DAVID WHEELER is associate professor and director of graduate studies in the English Department at the University of Southern Mississippi. Among his publications are essays on Alexander Pope, John Dennis, Joseph Warton, and Samuel Johnson in *The Scriblerian*, *Shakespeare Quarterly*, *South Central Review*, and *The British Journal for Eighteenth-Century Studies*.

INDEX

Abrams, M.H., 37, 147
Addison, Joseph: addiction to
  alcohol, 61; administrative
  competency of, 32; attitude
  toward poor, 59; *Battle of the
  Pygmies and Cranes*, 17; *Cato*,
  18; *The Drummer*, 52; on
  Milton, 115, 116; as moralist,
  20; on poetic style 21; as
  precursor of Johnson, 17;
  prose style, 18, 19, 22;
  Spectator, 115; timidity of, 33;
  Visions of Mirzah, 18; and
  War of Spanish Succession, 75
Adlerfeld, Gustave, 73
Alkon, Paul, 8, 60, 65
Altick, Richard, 27, 54-55
Augustus II (of Poland), 72
Austen, Jane, 23-24

Bachelard, Gaston, 89
Bacon, Sir Francis, 112
Bain, Robert Nisbet, 80
Barthes, Roland, 136
Bate, Walter Jackson, 4, 6, 16,
  17, 29, 141
Beattie, James, 53
Bentley, Richard, 116
Berkeley, George, 149
biography: and humanism, 26;

kinds of, 5; and probability,
  88-89; relationship with
  criticism, 6
Booth, Mark, 159-60
Booth, Wayne, 44-53
Boswell, James: as biographer
  of Johnson, 1-2; deficiencies
  as biographer, 5; on Johnson's
  thinking, 150
Brady, Frank, 139, 141
Burke, John J., Jr., 1, 154
Burroughs, Joseph, 65-66
Burrowes, Robert, 19

Catherine I (of Russia), 79
Cave, Edward, 154
Chapman, R.W., 77
Charles XII (of Sweden), 2,
  70-84; character of, 74; death
  of, 80-81; and fate, 79, 80; and
  Islam, 81-82; and Patkul
  affair, 78; religion of, 82
Chaucer, Geoffrey, 147
Chesterfield, Philip Dormer
  Stanhope, fourth Earl of, 74
Clifford, James, 153
Coleridge, Samuel Taylor, 19

Damrosch, Leopold, Jr., 8, 37,
  140, 153, 158, 159, 161, 162